Mirror, Mirror

Teen Girls Write About Body Image

By Youth Communication

Edited by Hope Vanderberg

YOUTH COMMUNICATION

True Stories by Teens

Mirror, Mirror

EXECUTIVE EDITORS
Keith Hefner and Laura Longhine

CONTRIBUTING EDITORS
Rachel Blustain, Clarence Haynes, Al Desetta, Andrea Estepa, Nora McCarthy, Kendra Hurley, Philip Kay, and Tamar Rothenberg

LAYOUT & DESIGN
Efrain Reyes, Jr. and Jeff Faerber

COVER ART
Isadora Versiani

ISBN 978-1-935552-00-0

Second, Expanded Edition

Printed in the United States of America

Youth Communication ®
New York, New York
www.youthcomm.org

Catalog Item #YD18-1

Table of Contents

Contents

When Nappy Didn't Make Me Happy

> Teased about her natural hair, Keshia subjects herself to
> the torture of straightening it.

Who's That Girl?

> Danny dresses as a girl for a day, and discovers what
> females have to deal with.

Cover Girl

> Bashiyrah is thrilled to be accepted at a modeling
> agency, but has mixed feelings about relying on
> modeling for her self-esteem.

I Was a Beauty School Sucker

> Tonya is taken in by an ad for a modeling school that
> appeals to her vanity.

Beauty or Beast?

> Angelina has mixed feelings about shaving her legs and
> underarms.

Trying Femininity on for Size

> Debbie goes from tomboy to girly flirt before she
> develops her own style.

Contents

Contents

Using the Book

Introduction

In a society obsessed with appearances, young women receive a variety of mixed messages about their bodies. These messages leap from the pages of magazines, ads, and commercials—and from the mouths of our own friends and family. They affect women of all ages, but they hit teen girls especially hard. That's because teens are going through a time of dramatic change, both in body and mind. They're busy trying to define themselves, and being told how to look by the media (and just as often by their peers) can make the journey to self-identity a difficult one. The result, as the young women in this book attest to in their stories, is confusion, emotional pain, and, in some cases, self-harm.

The young women writers in this book reflect on their struggles with body image with honesty, self-awareness, and sometimes humor. In "Big Breasts Are No Blessing," Rasheeda feels cursed by her large breasts and hates the attention they draw. In "My Cups Are Half-Empty," on the other hand, flat-chested Andrea longs to be more like "'Buxom Betty,' who got the guys, and less like 'Flat Felisha,' who got zip, zilch, nada." In the end, both try to be satisfied with what they've got, but haven't quite made peace with their bodies.

In many of the stories, body image is closely intertwined with race. The anonymous author of "Big, Black, and Beautiful" attends a white private school where blonde and thin is in. She's so uncomfortable with her "big butt" and curves that she transfers to another school. There, she's surprised to find black girls of all shapes and sizes who love their bodies, and she finally begins to accept her own.

The author of "Mirror, Mirror on the Wall" writes about bleaching her skin in an attempt to look more like her light-skinned mother. In "Lightening My Skin, Straightening My Hair," Samantha also uses skin bleach and perms to look like the light-skinned black models in the teen magazines she collects.

But eventually she gets so fed up that she ditches the magazines altogether. "I just couldn't bother with all the aggravation it took to try to be someone that I knew I wasn't and could never be," she writes.

Keshia, the author of "When Nappy Didn't Make Me Happy," comes to a similar conclusion. After fighting with her hair for years, she realizes she doesn't have to live up to anyone else's standards of beauty. "It wasn't me who didn't like my hair. It was the people who teased me, the sitcom actress, the girl on the magazine cover," she writes.

Many stories ask the question: Who decides what beautiful and feminine is? Angelina challenges the idea that girls have to shave their legs and underarms in her story, "Beauty or Beast?" And in "Trying Femininity on for Size," Debbie changes her clothing style from tomboyish to belly tops and heels, until she decides that, for her, feminine falls somewhere in the middle.

The stories in this book reveal the pain that many teen girls go through when it comes to body image. But the writers also show incredible strength as they begin to understand how their attitudes are influenced by society, and they attempt to fight against that pressure. As the first writer in this book says, "To be beautiful is one thing, but to feel beautiful is another. That was something I had to learn."

We hope that her story and the others in this book empower girls to challenge society's standards of beauty and decide for themselves what beauty is—and to find it in themselves.

In some stories, names and identifying details have been changed.

D. Alen Michailov

The Puberty Plague

By Marlene Peralta

When I was 11 and 12 years old, before I hit adolescence, I didn't care if I looked good or not. I just liked to have fun, and I was always running around, sweating, playing volleyball, and getting sunburned at the beach.

I was a very curious kid who liked to know everything that was happening around me. I used to ask so many questions. And I considered myself beautiful.

But when adolescence hit, so did some unhappy changes. When I was 14, my face started breaking out with pimples, and everything turned upside down. I started spending too much time thinking about my face and the way I looked.

The change was so drastic that I worried about every single thing about me. Having pimples made me worry if my shirt matched my skirt, or if my hair looked appropriate. It became an obsession, and I felt like the ugliest girl in the world.

It was terrible each time I looked at myself in the mirror with that face full of red marks.

"Look at my face," I used to say. "Why do I have pimples and my friends don't? Nobody will like me like this. I have to get rid of them."

One time a friend of mine was teaching a group of us how to use make-up because we were all going to participate in a fashion show. But when I put the foundation on my face, all my pimples became red.

I asked for help, and when my friend came to help me, she said, "There's no cure for you."

She meant it as a joke, but I felt so bad I wanted to cry. And I felt even worse when another friend told me the only way I could cure my problem was if I had plastic surgery!

In desperation, I began using every kind of remedy people recommended.

I've tried to remind myself of my good qualities and that appearance is not everything. I try to focus on the fact that I'm smart and do well in school, that I'm usually self-confident and strong. I'm a person who does not give up easily. Plus, I have a lot of great friends, and I like to make people feel good. It's rare to see me crying unless I'm laughing too much.

But it can be hard to remember those things with pimples covering my face. And when my face first started to break out, it was even harder.

When I was younger, I thought that being friends with attractive people was going to make me important. And I know I tend to assume that attractive people are mature and optimistic and that their personalities resemble their appearance.

So even though I didn't like being judged by my appearance, I also judged others by their appearance. And I judged myself, too. When I looked at myself in the mirror, it made me feel desperate and unable to do anything to stop the pimples.

It also made me feel guilty, because people kept telling me that my face was breaking out because I ate too much chocolate and butter, even though the main reason people's skin breaks out is because they're going through hormonal changes. My desperation turned to such an obsession that I began using every kind of remedy people recommended.

"You have a lot of pimples. Why don't you use hydrogen peroxide and mix it with lemon? It will dry up your face and take out all the pimples and blackheads," my mother's friend told me.

"Noxzema is a good cream to treat your pimples because it has alcohol that can help clean your face," a neighbor said.

I didn't care about my family's warnings: "Don't try everything that people tell you, it might make things worse." I just kept going with the remedies, hoping that I would be free of my plague.

I would wash my face three times in one hour (which actually is not good for your skin). And I tried at least seven different products. But they either dried my face too much or produced more pimples.

And I liked to pick my pimples to hurry the process of cleaning my face. But my face was getting holes in the places where I picked.

One time I put too much peroxide with lemon on my face because I thought it might speed things up. Instead, I just got more pimples. It was a terrible experience, but even though the results were so bad, I kept trying.

Because nothing was working, I grew more and more unhappy with my appearance, and this has affected my daily life. In some ways, I've stopped being the person who always had a smile on her face. It sounds stupid but it is true that pimples can make a person different.

One time I wanted to be in the school fashion show. But I

started thinking about my face, and I decided not to model.

And when I go to a party where I do not know anyone, guys and even girls often avoid me just because I have pimples. So I try to change my personality to fit in with them. Then it makes me feel mad at myself because I am pretending to be what I am not, and I think I shouldn't do it.

I've also learned to change in some good ways. Even though I feel more shy, I have learned to act confident and friendly. And this has helped me make friends.

Plus, having pimples has also made me more careful about how I judge people and how I choose my friends. I focus more on people's personalities than I used to.

Even though I feel more shy, I have learned to act more confident.

Before I had pimples, there were lots of guys who liked me; they were the kind of guys who like expensive clothes and are very vain. Now the guys who like me are cute, but they're also mature. They are not just looking for the most beautiful girl. They want girls who they relate to emotionally and who are able to take a relationship seriously.

But even though my attitude has changed in some ways, I still want to feel good about how I look. I do like my body and how clothes look on me. I also like my mouth and my long eyelashes. And sometimes when I get dressed up to go to a party, I like the way I look.

I want to take advantage of this. I want people to pay attention to me when I have to walk in front of them. I want to be a bright star before my batteries run out.

I think appearance is important because it is something that makes you feel good outside, and inside, too. But I also know that my friends and the guys who show interest in me like me for my whole self and because of who I am.

And even though I still value appearance, I also realize that it isn't everything, and that people who reject people with acne do not value the things that are really important.

Marlene was 17 when she wrote this story. She later got a master's degree in journalism and worked in Spanish-language television.

Yvonne Chen

Big Breasts Are No Blessing

By Rasheeda Raji

For years, I've had to deal with having big breasts. Many people tell me I'm lucky, that being busty is supposed to be a blessing. But I've found it difficult to be left alone because of this alleged gift.

Before I got these boobs, I enjoyed the easiness of being a child. Growing up, I wasn't into playing house or dress-up, or trying on make-up like other girls.

I wanted to be as much like my two older brothers as I could. Their interests became my interests because I didn't think they would like me if I were too girly.

So when they watched wrestling or other sporting events, I did too. When they played video games, so did I. I wanted them to think that I was a cool little sister. Somewhere in the back of my mind, I convinced myself that I was going to be a boy just like them.

That's why I was terribly disappointed when I started to develop. My new knockers kicked me out of my childhood and hurtled me into the beginning stages of womanhood. I started to develop when I was 11, although I denied that my body was changing until I was almost 13.

I refused to wear a training bra, insisting I didn't need one. My mother tried to talk me into getting one whenever we went shopping, but I always said "No!" or "What for?"

Getting a bra would've been an admission to myself that I was on my way to becoming a woman and being perceived in a sexual manner. By the time I reached the point where I agreed that I needed a bra, I was clear into a B cup. My first bra came from Victoria's Secret. I skipped training and went straight to work. (With my new development, I could now be employed by one of the best strip clubs in the city.)

I felt freakishly odd because people started to make comments about my chest. I wasn't comfortable with strangers looking at me sexually. It was awkward to think about the vulgar thoughts I knew some guys were starting to have.

Until I turned 15, I wore oversized clothing to hide my boobs.

Once, I was just hanging around a bunch of male friends when one of them blurted out, "Got Milk?" At first I laughed, because I can laugh at myself every once in a while. But that joke lost its humor well before the millionth time.

I felt like an object, not a person, and, even worse, I felt like a slut. Guys that I had known for most of my life were making me feel cheap and dirty.

And it hurt even more when my relatives made thoughtless comments. At a family gathering, my aunt said I could knock somebody out with my hooters. I cried for hours after that.

I thought it was mean to pick on a young girl in front of family members, but my aunt thought it was just good-natured teasing and I was too sensitive. She's a model, and her life revolves around her body. She thought it was great that my breasts were so large, since I could show off my body and get tons of attention, like she did.

But her idea that everyone enjoys being ogled was incorrect. I wanted to be a wallflower and left alone. I didn't want anybody staring at me.

Others in my family teased me about my breasts as well. I detested the constant ridicule, and I didn't enjoy being the subject of jokes at family reunions. It was extremely embarrassing.

After a couple of years, I learned to push the comments to the back of my mind. I got sick of crying about every remark. No one seemed to care and the tears weren't doing a thing for me.

Instead, I tried to make myself feel better in other ways. Until I turned 15, I wore big, oversized clothing to hide my boobs. My wardrobe consisted of floppy sweatshirts and T-shirts since I didn't bother to look in the female section when I went shopping.

No one seemed to care that I only wore men's clothes, that I looked like a fat guy. I was temporarily happy, because despite looking like I'd stolen one of my big brother's outfits, my boobs didn't look so big. I didn't have to deal with the perverts who usually gazed in wonder.

But three years ago, when I was 15, I had a revelation. One night, when I was at my best friend's house, she asked me why I always covered up. She thought I was ashamed of my body. I told her I wasn't, and I just happened to like baggy clothes.

Honestly, I was ashamed, but in denial. I didn't realize that until she pointed it out to me. I covered up because I was embarrassed about the size of my breasts.

A couple of hours after leaving her house, I realized I was sick of always looking like a boy. I thought to myself, "I'm not a guy, and God made me this way, so why should I be ashamed?"

I'm a girl and there's nothing wrong with me looking like one, at least every once in a while. So now I attempt to look more girly at least once a week, even though that can be quite the chore.

But I was still sensitive about my bustiness. That's why I attempted to maintain some distance from boys. I went to an all-girls high school freshmen year because I didn't want to deal with guys. After that I was home-schooled. I also didn't date. I couldn't tell if a guy was really interested in me or my DDs, so I didn't bother trying to figure it out.

Thankfully, by the time I was 16, my male and female friends were more sensitive to my feelings. It became common knowledge that my breasts weren't to be discussed. They remembered the crying spells and rages I'd had over people talking about them in the past.

But, to this day, I must deal with comments that I wish people would have enough sense not to say. At every family function (which I can't seem to avoid), there's still at least one remark on the size of my breasts. I even caught a guidance counselor talking about them in Spanish as if I wasn't in the room.

Why don't people understand that casually talking about my chest isn't OK? And shouldn't folks know that it's not appropriate to ask, "What size are those things anyway?" or, "Don't those things hurt?"

I realized I was sick of always looking like a boy.

I don't see how that's anyone's business but mine, but I still answer the idiotic questions. It's easier for me to tell people what they want to know, since they usually leave me alone once they've gotten the information.

I'm puzzled when someone says, "I wish I were your size." Why would anyone want something the size of honeydews hanging from her body? Why would anyone want the first thing people associated with them to be their breasts?

Some people have suggested I get a breast reduction, but I don't like the idea of unnecessary surgery, so that's out of the question for now. If I develop unbearable back pain in the future, though, then I'd consider the operation.

And even though I complain, after having my breasts for the last seven years, I've gotten used to them. I'm not happy about them, but they're here. The extreme embarrassment that I once felt has died down to annoyance.

The shame isn't totally gone. It pops up on occasion. But I know my bust-line isn't going anywhere, even though I wish the comments would.

Rasheeda was 18 when she wrote this story.
She is currently in law school at Howard University.

Patricia Battles

My Cups Are Half-Empty

By Andrea Guscott

I've always been the girl whose chest is as flat as the plank on a pirate's ship. My 34A bra size hasn't changed much since my fun-bags first sprouted in 5th grade. They're the same old ice cream cone-shaped breasts (without the double scoop) that they've always been. I'm coping with them now, but there were times when they drove me nuts.

My mother unselfishly passed her flat chest on to my two sisters and me. I do commend her for her willingness to share, but I think my grandma's secret recipe for stewed chicken would have been a better choice.

I was able to talk to my mom about my flat chest because she suffered from the same affliction. But she bummed me out when she told me that none of the breast-enhancing products that I'd seen advertised really worked.

I went from 5th grade to junior high with my unmistakably underdeveloped boobs. It was as if two alien life forms had latched onto my chest and decided to protrude only a few inches outward before stopping.

In junior high, it seemed like everyone had some cleavage: my friends, my teacher "Ms. Boobington," even the dean—and he was a man. I just couldn't escape those oversized mammary glands that everyone else had.

And I noticed that the media always publicized and encouraged big knockers. I wanted to have them too, just to fit in. Finally, I decided to take my melons into my own hands. I was going to make them bigger.

> *It seemed like everyone had some cleavage: my friends, my teacher, even the dean—and he was a man.*

Stuffing my bra was out of the question in 6th grade, because the kids at school had already seen my flat chest. I had to make it seem like it had grown on its own. I decided to ask the one person I knew who was struggling as badly as I was—my twin sister.

She told me about a suggestion she'd gotten from her friend. I was supposed to massage my twins in a circular motion. I doubted it would work, but I tried it anyway.

I did it every day for 30 seconds and soon, to my surprise (or more correctly, to my delusion), it seemed as if my bust had gotten bigger.

But it turned out my eyes were playing tricks on me. One day my chest would look bigger and the next day it would look the same as before. I realized I'd let my eagerness for larger boobs get the best of me. I wanted bigger hooters so I saw myself with them. As it turned out, they were still small.

Not long after my big-boob mission failed, I saw an ad in a catalog at my house for some pills that were supposed to enhance bust size. I couldn't order them because I didn't have any money. And asking my parents for cash to make my bongos grow didn't seem like an option. My quest to make Thelma and Louise larger didn't end, but it was put on hold.

By 8th grade, my bazookas still hadn't grown an inch. Most of the girls in my school had bigger breasts than me. I began to notice that the girls with the real grab bags got all the attention from the guys.

I wanted some attention too, even if it was negative, like construction workers hollering at a pretty woman walking down the street. I wanted acknowledgment for my honkers, too.

I was tired of guys comparing my chest to an ironing board, or holding a sheet of paper next to my chest and saying, "Look, twins." I wanted to be more like "Buxom Betty," who got the guys, and less like "Flat Felisha," who got zip, zilch, nada.

In 8th grade, I started to like a guy in my class. We started talking, and pretty soon he found out I liked him. He gladly welcomed my advances. He saw how flat I was, but he never said anything about my breasts. When we started dating, his acceptance of me and my body made me realize that a large chest isn't that important.

In fact, I think that if he'd seen my self-consciousness, he wouldn't have dated me. I learned that my love cushions didn't define me. They were just a tiny part of who I was (no pun intended).

But even now, in my senior year of high school, I haven't totally stopped obsessing about my cones. Just last week I was looking at yet another ad on the Internet about some medication to increase my bust size. I only held off on purchasing it because I don't have a credit card.

I still want bigger breasts and I don't think that desire will burn out any time soon. But tatas are tatas, and I'm trying to be satisfied with the ones I've got. If they don't get bigger, it won't be the end of the world. Besides, skinny girls are in now, so I plan to have a little fun while my ladies are in style.

Andrea was 17 when she wrote this story. She later attended college, studying public policy.

Elizabeth Deegan

Big, Black, and Beautiful

By Anonymous

It took me a long time to convince myself that I am a beautiful girl.

I grew up going to a private school where I was one of only a few black students. At that school, it seemed like only the thin, blond, and big-chested girls were considered appealing.

I am 5'7" and weigh 150 lbs. I am truly a brick house and have been called thick many times. No matter how fit I was, people regularly commented on my size because I wasn't thin and didn't look like a supermodel.

Some students would talk about my round butt, thick hair and lips and shapely figure. "Nobody wants your fat butt," one guy told me.

I constantly worried about my physical appearance as a result. Whenever I'd get around friends I'd ask, "How does my hair look?" or, "Do I look fat in this outfit?" I was becoming almost annoying.

Because of the comments about my body, I often felt hurt, sad, and angry. Even if my friends and family told me how pretty, smart, or popular I was, the weight slurs would go straight to my head.

I'd try to defend myself, but that would only make them bother me even more. They knew the slurs would hurt me, even if what they said was not true.

I felt so bad about myself that when attractive black guys looked at me, I'd turn my head and look the other way. I thought I knew what they wanted—white girls, Hispanic girls, or light-skinned black girls with long legs and straight hair.

But at the same time, I'd get whistles and catcalls from black and Hispanic guys on the street who said complimentary things about my body. I'd wonder why they bothered. I was the big girl, the fat one.

> *I thought I knew what guys wanted—white girls, Hispanic girls, or light-skinned black girls with long legs and straight hair.*

It hurt the most when the boys would call me fat. Most of the guys in my school were white. The ones who weren't liked white girls, or at least the girls who looked like white girls. And since there weren't many black guys in my school, I wanted to please the white guys and look and act the way they wanted me to.

A great thing about my school was that I could date guys of different races and no one would stare or say a thing, because everybody dated each other. But because I dated white guys, my friends outside of school called me a "white girl." They didn't like that I dated out of my race.

And I felt it was not exactly normal, because when my white boyfriends and I would go out to the movies or the mall, we'd get stares. One time an old boyfriend and I were waiting in the train station. A Hispanic guy started to sing "Jungle Fever," a Stevie

Wonder song about interracial couples.

My boyfriend and I just looked at each other and started to laugh. But it wasn't funny. It wasn't anyone's business what we did.

*E*ven though I tried to look and act like a white girl with my friends from school, when I hung out with friends outside of school I had to try and act cool, maybe even throw in some slang. But I sounded so stupid that I got picked on even more.

I was always called the "white girl" whenever I was around my family or my black friends who didn't go to my school.

"Do you think you have thin lips?" or "Why do you fling your hair like that?" they would ask.

I'd try to ignore their comments, which were about everything from my legs to my hair. But it was hard.

Once, when a friend noticed I was shaving my legs, she looked at me disapprovingly and said, "Black girls don't shave their legs!"

I asked her what she meant by that and she said, "Black guys think hairy legs are sexy." I don't think that's always true, or that it even matters.

My friend also told me that "respectable black women don't show off their stomachs either." Why couldn't she just ask me not to wear that shirt because she didn't like it, instead of making it into a race issue?

I felt as though one day couldn't pass without my friends and family mocking something I did that was totally natural for me. They made a race issue out of my looks, my voice, how I pronounced words, and everything I did.

Their remarks always offended me. What did they mean, talking like a white girl? It was ridiculous! I was proud of the education I got at my school. I didn't know how to talk or act in any other way.

It was horrible. The more I strived to speak like an educated person, the more I was considered a white girl by my own race.

I know it doesn't have to be that way. Last summer I visited Spelman College, a historically black women's college in Atlanta, Georgia. The alumni there were extremely smart and had perfect diction.

They were also proud of being black and were sure of their culture. They showed me that a black person can be and sound educated without losing her black identity. But in my old school, and with my friends and family, that didn't seem to be the case.

Finally, I got fed up and decided to transfer to a different school. I was tired of being examined and analyzed by everyone.

Shortly after I arrived at my new high school, I began to have a whole new outlook on life. I noticed girls of all different sizes had boyfriends, and fine ones, too.

"How did she get him? Look at her size," I would think. Walking the halls, guys commented on girls' butts—but not the way I was used to.

"Look at how round it is, that's so fly," they'd say.

I was really shocked. These guys liked big butts and girls like me? Wow!

I began to forget about my looks and could concentrate on my schoolwork. I knew I had to get my head together, or else. I began to boost up my grades, receive awards, and get asked on trips. I felt really good about myself because I was able to use education as a way to build myself up. Once my marks rose, I felt great.

At the new school, no one commented on the way I talked, acted or dressed. I was kind of expecting them to say something, but they didn't. I'm not sure if I was losing my "white girl" character, or if they just didn't care.

After a while, I began to compare myself to other black females in my life. Many of my black girl friends love themselves, regardless of what size they are.

Where did they get such positive attitudes? My white girl friends from the private school continuously complained about their size and thought they had to be thin to be accepted by men.

It would be great if more white girls had the same positive body image as many black girls. It also would be great if black girls would feel good about showing how educated they are, and would take a lesson from successful black women like the alumni I met at Spelman. Speaking and acting educated doesn't have anything to do with being white or black.

I found out I don't have to look like a white girl or talk like a black girl. It may be best to be right in the middle.

The author was 17 when she wrote this story. She gradauted from college and got a master's degree in urban affairs.

Elizabeth Deegan

Lightening My Skin, Straightening My Hair

By Samantha Brown

When I was 10 years old, I wanted to see everything and be everything. That meant having phat clothing, a great body, a lot of friends, and a fine cutie on one arm.

I used to collect teen magazines and sit for hours at night reading their quizzes and hair-care tips, and envying the models. These girls seemed too perfect to be true. Every one of my friends wanted to be like them.

While we still wore our hair in four, they were already primping and perming. While we were still playing with Ken and Barbie, they were wearing bras, having serious relationships, and battling the problems of sex.

My addiction to teen magazines didn't reach its full height until I entered junior high. I looked to them to help me get a man, learn how to kiss and master the rules of dating. I believed if I got the proper training from these magazines, I would be set for life.

For most of this time, it never really bothered me that the teen models were mostly white, or that the black teens who did appear tended to be light-skinned with long, soft, curly hair. My friends weren't fazed by this either. We just accepted it as if it were normal.

One of my friends even said she hoped to marry a white guy so that her children would have pretty hair. Another friend would go around bragging that she was light-skinned and if anyone had anything to say about it, then they were just jealous.

I wanted to be accepted, and I thought I would be if I had lighter skin and straighter hair like most of the black models in the teen magazines that we looked to as the ideal of black beauty.

So I began a beauty routine to lighten my complexion and straighten my hair. I used skin cream to make my complexion lighter. I would buy 16-ounce bottles for about $4 a piece and plaster it all over my face every night. For a while this strategy appeared to be working—my complexion was a little lighter and people even commented on it. But when I ran out of money, I also ran out of skin cream.

Then I began begging my mother to let me get a perm. The first time I permed my hair was at home. My sister did the honors.

I waited almost an hour to get my hair straight, but when it was finally finished, my hair was still a little nappy. Whenever my sister would perm my hair, the perm would only stay in for about four days (as long as I didn't wash it). I began to think my sister's perms were useless, so I pleaded with my mother to let me go to a salon.

For a while she let me get a regular perm like everyone else— but this didn't last. My mother didn't want to pay $45 every six weeks for something that she objected to and that was damaging my hair.

By the time I was a freshman in high school, I had begun to

think that I would never fit the image of the light-complexioned teen with soft, curly hair. Feeling frustrated about changing my looks, I began to question whether I was really the one who needed the change.

I began to feel frustrated, too, at how caught up I had let myself get in these magazines and how caught up my friends still were. After a while, instead of reading the articles, I found myself counting the number of whites compared to the number of non-whites. This was almost a daily ritual. My friends thought that I was crazy. A friend of mine who is half Indian and half black would say I was just jealous—she never understood why I was so upset.

But, like me, most of my friends felt that they weren't perfect enough and that their look wasn't acceptable. Lots of times they tried to correct these so-called problems by perming their hair, putting on a lot of makeup, and living in denial of their true identities—just like I had.

I thought I would never fit the image of the light-complexioned teen with soft, curly hair.

Now I'm 17 and I've hardly read any teen magazines in almost three years. I just couldn't bother with all the aggravation it took to try to be someone that I knew I wasn't and could never be. And I wasn't going to waste my time and money reading magazines that weren't interested in me.

Sometimes I do miss reading quizzes like "10 Love Lies," and "Is He the One for You?" There are times when I wish that I could forget about being left out and just lie back on my bed and read a funny story or check out the fashion do's and don'ts. But until I can open up a teen magazine and see a dark-skinned girl with her hair in dreads or just natural, with her 10 dark-skinned friends standing next to her, I'll have to get my laughs from the funnies.

Samantha was 17 when she wrote this story. She later graduated from the University of Michigan.

Karolina Zaniesienko

When Nappy Didn't Make Me Happy

By Keshia Harrell

It was November of 5th grade, and my mother and I were in the hair supply store. As we walked up the hair-straightening aisle, I figured this was as good a time as any.

"Mom, can I get a perm?"

"Perm? What you want a perm for?"

"To make my hair straight."

"Girl, you don't need no perm. Your hair is fine."

"But all the other girls in my class have perms and I don't want to be the only one with kinky hair."

"Your hair isn't kinky. It's curly and it's natural."

"OK," I sulked. I wasn't going to win this argument.

I felt like the only girl in 5th grade without straight hair. Mom usually did my hair in ponytails. She sometimes braided my puffy ends and left a swoop of remaining hair falling on my right cheek and three little braids in the front covering my big forehead. Other times she'd box braid my hair all over.

But I went to a school where the majority of students were white or Hispanic, most with long hair. Some had naturally straight hair. But even the white and Hispanic girls who had curly hair straightened their hair.

They made me feel like I wasn't as pretty as they were because my hair wasn't as long or as straight. They made comments about my "short and kinky" hair. Some girls asked me, "Why is it like that?" Like it was abnormal. I told myself that they didn't know what they were talking about. But in 5th grade, the few girls in my school with kinky hair got perms to straighten it. Some wore it with a part in the middle and curled under at the ends. Others wore it half up, with the back out and drop curls at the ends.

"Why don't you get a perm?" some girls occasionally asked me. I felt left out.

On top of that, every magazine I saw for black females made me feel like I had to have straight hair too. I resembled the sad girl in some ad's "before" picture. And even though my mom said my hair looked fine natural, the smiling girl with her new and improved permed hair in the "after" picture succeeded in making me feel like my kind of hair wasn't acceptable.

"When this is all over, I'll be pretty," I thought.

Mom or Grandma would press my hair to make it straight on special occasions, like picture day at school or friends' birthday parties.

Grandma would stand over the stove, heating up the black metal hot comb over the fire. After testing how hot the comb was so it wouldn't burn my hair, she'd pull it through a section of my hair with a clear hair grease. My hair was soon straight and slick.

The following year, the pressure increased. When I began 6th grade in my new junior high, my classmates teased me about my wild hair.

"Yo, Keshia, you'd be pretty if you did something with your hair," one of the boys in my class told me.

"You look like an African!" said Mareena, one of my classmates. "It's so kinky."

"I am African," I told her. "African-American."

"No, you look like you're straight from Africa."

"OK," I thought. Was I supposed to take that as an insult? Africa is where my ancestors are from.

Despite her ignorance, Mareena's comment hurt. I felt like an ugly outcast. That night, I nearly came to tears as I thought about what she'd said. But I told myself, "Don't cry. Only the weak cry. Their words and thoughts don't affect me."

I was hurt that I was being judged by something so trivial, but I wanted to be accepted. So I tried again to convince my mother and grandmother to let me get a perm or relaxer.

"No, Keshia, you don't need a perm. Do you want your hair to fall out? Then you won't have to worry about getting a perm," Grandma said.

"OK," I pouted. But I still wanted straight, flowing hair like Keshia Knight Pulliam, who played Rudy, one of the daughters on *The Cosby Show*.

Then a couple of months later, my aunt asked me to be a bridesmaid in her wedding. At the wedding, all my female cousins and aunts were talking about how much easier it was to have a perm. I guess that influenced my grandma and mother, because before we went back to New York, I got my hair permed.

I was so happy to be sitting in that big black leather salon chair. "When this is all over, I'll be pretty," I thought. "No one will make fun of me."

I closed my eyes as the beautician matted the chemical-smelling white cream into my hair. After a couple of minutes, though, I felt a burning sensation on my scalp. "It's burning!" I screamed. It felt as if the perm was eating my hair out from the roots. The beautician hurried over and started to rinse the cream out.

I saw a few patches of hair in the sink. A little more came out as she combed. But it was all worth it to me. My hair was straight.

The beautician pulled my hair into a bun, stuffing it to make it look big. I was happy. I went back to school thinking, "Finally I'm going to fit in with the rest of the girls."

"Keshia, you finally got your hair permed," they said. I was ecstatic about not being teased anymore. Even the boys noticed.

"It's about time you did something with your hair," some said. I told them to shut up.

After two weeks of straight hair, I realized that my perm wasn't as glorious as I thought it would be. I felt a little worse about myself because I'd changed to be accepted by others. Plus, after I took my bun out, my hair was straight at the roots and puffed out and frizzy at the ends. I wanted to scream. My hair still wasn't straight.

"What happened to your ends?" my classmates asked. "Whoever permed your hair didn't leave it in long enough."

"Shut up!" I wanted to scream.

No matter how much I conditioned or put a flat iron through my hair, it still frizzed up. And my mother and grandmother decided against letting me keep my hair permed because of hair breakage and the burns. But I still wanted my hair to be straight. So when my perm grew out, I decided to learn how to use the hot comb on my own.

I lost a lot of hair trying to use the hot comb. I had a habit of leaving it on the stove for too long and not testing it. I'd put the comb to my hair and hear a sizzling sound followed by the pungent smell of burnt hair. I'd look in the mirror and want to cry. Once, I singed my hair so badly that I ended up losing a big chunk of hair from the middle of my head. That was enough of hot combs for me.

So I taught myself to braid. At first, my braids came out crooked and bushy at the ends, but I got better since I also used my little sister's hair to practice. (She didn't mind.) People still made comments about my hair. "I like your hair," some said. "You didn't braid it tight enough," others said.

For a while, the positive comments made me feel good. And the negative comments didn't hurt as much as they did before. I was becoming a little more confident in myself, so their opinions didn't matter as much.

Still, on my first day of high school, it felt like all the girls had just walked out of a beauty parlor. They had wraps, weaves, braids and curls. My hair was in a semi-straight, semi-frizzy ponytail on top of my head. I felt like an outcast once again.

So, for most of my freshman and sophomore year, I suffered through hot comb and curlers.

At the beginning of my junior year, I was looking in the mirror thinking of how I was going to do my hair for the first day of school. Suddenly, I got sick. Sick of burning myself. Sick of having to get up in the morning to do it. Sick of my hair frizzing up when it was rainy or humid. Sick of worrying about what people would think of it. Sick of conforming to make other people happy.

Whose standards of beauty say you have to have straight hair to be beautiful? Not mine.

So I started to braid it again. Accepting my puffs was hard. I'd get up in the morning and look in the mirror and worry about what people would think. Even now I have to repeatedly remind myself that I shouldn't worry about what others think and that if I like my hairstyle, then that's all that matters.

Now I'm a senior, and people still stare at me because of my hair and ask, "Why don't you do something with it?" I do my hair depending on my mood. If I'm tired and I don't care, I leave my Afro-puff in a ponytail on top of my head. (People have compared it to a bird's nest, but I've grown to love it.) Other times I braid it. And sometimes when I get bored with my puffs and braids, I press my hair, just for a different look.

After years of looking in the mirror and getting upset about my reflection, I realized that it wasn't me who didn't like my hair. It was the people who teased me, the sitcom actress, the girl on the magazine cover.

Now I know that I don't have to be beautiful in the societal sense; I can be beautiful in the me sense. I don't look like every other girl in my school, and I like it that way.

Sometimes, though, I still feel ugly because of my hair, like when I read Ebony or CosmoGirl magazine. But then I think, "Whose standards of beauty say you have to have straight hair to be beautiful?" Not mine. That makes me feel better.

I no longer have daydreams of looking like Keshia Knight Pulliam; I'd rather look like Keshia LaToria Harrell. Myself.

Keshia was 17 when she wrote this story.
She later attended college.

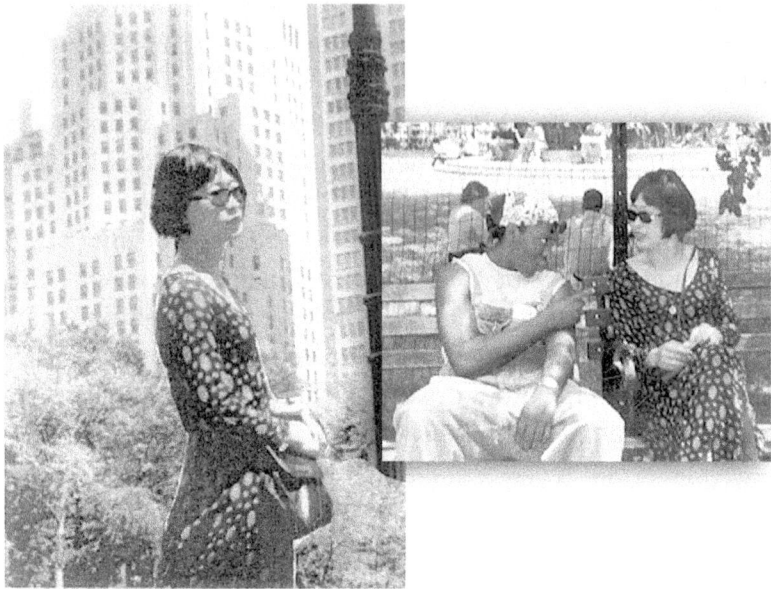

YC Art Dept.

Who's That Girl?

By Danny Gong

So, guys, you thought taking off a bra was hard? Well you haven't tried nothing till you've tried putting one on. I would know, because, well…I did.

Nooo, this was not my idea. And no, it wasn't because I like trying on my mother's clothes! I just wanted to write about how people stare and criticize the way other people look—like me, for example, 'cause my hair is always sticking up straight. I wanted to investigate how the way you dress—and the way people react to you—affects the way you feel.

But Rachel, my editor at the teen magazine I write for, thought that I wasn't weird enough as is, and that I should do something even more crazy. As we sat pondering what we could do to spice up the story, my other editor, Nora, casually said, "Why don't you wear a dress? People will definitely stare. Ha ha ha."

Thanks to that "casual comment," Rachel asked me if I would do it.

At first I was mortified at the thought, but then I thought, "OK, it's for the sake of the article. I'll do it." After all, I figured, men in the Renaissance wore dresses. Why shouldn't we? And that's how we decided I would venture out to see what it felt like to dress like a girl, and find out how girls feel when guys check them out.

A few times I had serious second thoughts. But finally the morning came when I was going to wear the dress outside. Changing in the bathroom, I tugged on the navy blue dress with flowers and somehow it fit. Then I looked down at myself. "You gotta be kidding me," I thought. Man was this dress cut low. "I'm gonna need some breasts, too!"

When I came out of the bathroom, Rachel said, "Wow, you look really good in that dress. It looks better on you than on my sister."

I mumbled in response. What could I say? Al, another editor, started to pretend to hit on me. Mimi, a teen writer, walked in, took one look at me and started to giggle. But I didn't care if they laughed. I was laughing too.

Lots of times I've seen girls check out their makeup and hair in store windows. Now I understood why.

I returned to the bathroom and tried on a chin-length black wig. I put on the bra (after a few tips). While I was putting it on, I heard someone shout, "Ahhh!" It was Nora. I had forgotten to lock the bathroom door. After I stuffed the bra with toilet paper and opened the door to leave, my right boob got caught on the door. I freed myself and walked out.

It was time for lipstick and mascara. Mimi helped me put on the lipstick, called Kiss Me Red. "I think you should have shaved this morning," she said.

"I can't believe I'm doing this," I thought. I had to keep telling myself, "It's for the article, Danny, for the article!" Then it was show time.

I left the office with a black purse, and Mimi, Kelvin, and Zizi, three other members of the teen staff. I walked outside, where it was warm, sunny, and everyone could see me. And at that moment it felt like a dream. Nothing seemed real.

Then somehow it hit me, and suddenly I was totally embarrassed. But I relaxed after a few moments. I felt comfortable wearing my men's black dress shoes (we didn't know any women with feet my size), and most people didn't really seem to notice me. Well, not yet at least.

We headed downtown. While we walked, I started to worry about how I presented myself in public. I passed a deli and pretended to look through a window as if I were thinking about going in. Instead, I looked at my reflection.

Mainly I wanted to make sure I had a feminine appearance. But I also wanted to know if I still looked fine!

Lots of times I've seen girls check out their makeup and hair in store windows. Now I understood why. When you're dressed as a girl, there are just more things to worry about.

I was also worrying about how I walked. I had to make my butt protrude more and my hips had to sway from side to side so the dress could move in sequence when I did the walk. Any other walk and it would have lost its flow.

After a while, it seemed like more people began to notice me. Men stared at me as if they thought I was a woman. It was gross, and a little hilarious. They'd turn their heads like they do when a girl walks by. I thought to myself, "Oh boy, if they only knew what was really under this dress, they would freak out."

My friends, who were walking behind me, told me that one guy was checking out my butt for a block and a half. "Pervert!" I thought. (Although I guess in some ways it could be a compliment. Six years of Rollerblading is bound to shape up anyone's butt.)

Anyway, after walking around as a girl for a while, I can tell you that being checked out by a guy is way different from being checked out by a girl. Guys look below the neck and, from what I've seen, girls look above it.

Girls kind of look back and forth from time to time, while guys stare wide-eyed like owls. The girls' techniques are playful. As for guys, no matter how good looking you may be, if you stare too long she's going to think you're a stalker.

The nasty thing I discovered is that it's less young guys who stare and more old ugly men. Most of the guys who looked at me were old enough to be my father.

After a while we went to Union Square Park in Manhattan. An old man was singing the blues and playing his harmonica, and when he saw me he smiled and started to sing to me. That was kind of cool.

Soon we left, walked some more, grabbed some lunch, and got on the subway back to the office. I had gotten bored of playing with the fake voice so I just spoke in my regular voice. I said to Kelvin, "I can't wait till I get into my normal clothes." The dress was killing me!

One guy looked at me and began to mumble. Another guy in a business suit kept staring at me like he was going to kill me. As I exited the crowded train, I said, "Excuse me" very loudly. Boy did that turn heads.

I really just wanted to find out what it was like to be a girl, but I got a little taste of what it's like to be a drag queen, too. Let me tell you, it's not easy.

The next day, back at the office, I typed up everything that had happened. At last, I thought, I'll be able to relax.

Boy was I was wrong, because then my editor came over and told me that now I had to figure out what this all meant. At that point I went completely insane trying to analyze being a girl. Boy are they complex. But this is what I came up with.

I think that nature, the media, guys, and girls are all responsible for the fact that girls are expected to focus more on their appearance than guys are. Girls are also expected to be more passive when it comes to asking guys out, so they have to do something to attract our attention.

But whatever the reasons, I think having to worry so much about their appearance all the time makes girls less assertive when it comes to relationships, and maybe other things, too. They have other things to worry about instead of making the first move—like the way they walk or who they can attract.

It's not like I don't worry about my appearance when I'm dressed like a guy. I definitely do. For instance, I try to style my hair in a way that makes me look good and catches attention.

I think having to worry so much about their appearance all the time makes girls less assertive when it comes to relationships.

But when I was dressed as a girl, I just had so many more things to check on. Like if I had lipstick on my teeth. If the mascara was smudging. Not to mention, I had the extra problem of the wig, too. If I had been at a party, I just would have been too busy to make the first move with anyone.

Besides, when girls are dressed nicely, the guys usually go up to them. So they don't need to go after what they want.

Dressing pretty does give females some power, just like how a man would wear a suit to get more respect. It's like beauty-power. If they have a lot of guys who look at them, then they have a greater variety to choose from. And guys are more polite and do nice little things for them just because they look the way they do. Look at the guy who played his harmonica for me in the park. That probably would never have happened if I hadn't looked so fine.

But it makes girls less powerful, too, because somehow when you're worrying so much about how you look, and everyone's always expecting you to look nice, you just aren't as aggressive as you might be.

From my three-hour experience dressed in drag, I also learned the mistakes that guys make when they look at a girl. I understand why some girls wouldn't even bother to talk to guys in the street, because it gets annoying being checked out like a piece of meat all the time.

Even though I thought it was fun to cross dress, I wouldn't do it again unless I had to. I like wearing my pants. And I'd much, much, much rather have girls checking out my buns than a bunch of old geezers.

Danny was 18 and a senior in high school when he wrote this story. He graduated from college and now teaches American Sign Language in Japan.

Rosa Perin

Cover Girl

By Bashiyrah Morrow

In junior high school, when I used to tell my friends I wanted to be a model, they would laugh at me. They said I wasn't pretty enough and I wasn't tall enough. At least, they said, I sure had the attitude. You know that sulky, serious attitude that models have.

People thought I had a bad attitude because I didn't smile. I didn't have a bad attitude. It's just that no matter how hard I tried to smile, it wouldn't come out unless someone made me laugh.

For a lot of years my life was pretty serious. Living with my aunt and not my mother was getting me down. I was in a depression when I should have been going on swings in the park. I was serious while everyone else was jolly. My life just didn't seem to fit.

But when I watched models on TV, they were so pretty, and their lives seemed so exciting. It seemed wonderful to have people want to know everything about you, for your beauty to make them turn their heads. I'd think, "I want to be on TV, too. I want to be a star."

In my real life though, most people didn't see me as any kind of star. Sure, my family told me I was pretty and could be a model, but the kids in school treated me more like an outcast.

I did have a couple of friends, but often, when the bell rang for lunch, I'd go outside with a little book and a pen and draw or write. I was a goody-two-shoes, too, and I answered most questions in class. Because of all these things, most of the other girls in school didn't like me much.

The popular girls in my class would laugh loudly and look my way. They'd make little comments like, "That ugly b-tch," or, "She can't dress." I knew they were talking about me because I sat nowhere near anybody else.

When they insulted me, I just keep telling myself I wasn't ugly, I knew I wasn't a b-tch, and I could dress, even though I didn't have much. Still, back then I was soft. Any insult would make me cry, not in public but in the bathroom at home where no one could see.

The models I saw on TV were so pretty, and their lives seemed so exciting.

When I got into high school, I stopped caring as much about what people said. There was no more crying and no more of Mama asking where all the tissues went. In part, my attitude changed because a couple of really nice boys started paying attention to me, and that made all the horrible names the girls had been calling me hurt less.

Plus, I got my first job, and every time I got paid, I'd buy myself little tins of makeup. At first I only used lip liner and lip gloss, but I had all the colors. I also started to take care of the pimples that had come with puberty, and to treat my hair with care because I was tired of looking like some wild adolescent.

Soon I added black shadow to my eyelids. I saved my money and bought clothes that were in style. I gained a little weight and was no longer so skinny. I was getting prettier and prettier.

The girls and boys who used to tease me didn't even recognize me as I walked down the street with my head raised high. The boys would be sitting on street corner boxes smoking weed and, when I passed, they'd make all kinds of sounds like I was a cat. I thought to myself, "Who's the average girl now?"

*B*ut all this focus on how I looked was getting a little out of control. Sometimes I was late for school because I needed my makeup. You couldn't get me outside without it. Other times I couldn't concentrate in class because I was worrying so much about how I looked. A lot of the work that I used to do with no problem, I didn't get done anymore.

I thought that if I really became a model, I wouldn't have to worry so much about whether I was pretty. I'd know for sure.

That spring, I found an ad in the newspaper. They wanted girls over 5'3".

I'm only 5'4", so I've always known I could never be a runway model. But I've read a lot about modeling, and knew I could be in commercials, or on boxes for things like hair dyes.

I thought that this would be my chance. My chance to show everybody and myself that I am beautiful. My mother called the agency and they scheduled me a meeting the next week.

When my mother and I got there, I had butterflies in my stomach and my mouth was dry. And when I got into the waiting room, God knows I wanted to cry. All the girls looked 6' or taller. I was in shock.

I wanted to leave but I knew my mother would be angry, so I stayed. They called six of us into a room and asked us to walk down the runway. There were like 20 people watching. I was nervous, but I had to think big because I knew this was my chance to accomplish my goal.

The two girls ahead of me did great. Then it was my turn to show those seven judges that I was the star. I walked up to the floor, lifted my head and just flowed. It felt like I walked at least a mile; the runway never seemed to end. When I finished, I tried to remain all calm and chic, but my heart was racing and I made a beeline for the bathroom. I needed air so I could breathe again. When I returned to the room, they told everyone not to call, that they would call us. But after seeing those other girls, I thought, "What would they want with me?"

Three days passed without a call. My life was over. Then the phone rang while I was at my boyfriend's house. It was my mother. I was accepted into the agency, she said. They had only accepted 35 out of 130 girls, and I was one of them!

I was so excited I didn't know what to do. I kept thinking about seeing myself on TV and about other people seeing me too.

Unfortunately, now that I've started modeling school, I don't love it so much. I still want to have my face displayed all over. But there are a number of things I don't like.

I don't like the diet. Every time you go there they check to see whether you've gained weight, and that makes me self-conscious. Some of the classes are cheesy, too. They try to teach you self-esteem while they're telling you everything about yourself you need to fix. Plus, I don't love that I have to pay $60 a week for 20 weeks. There's only one class a week, and classes only last two and a half hours.

And it hasn't fixed everything like I thought it would. When I'm back home, I no longer feel as beautiful as I do at the modeling school. I feel like I'm right back to my regular self. I still worry all the time whether I'm pretty enough. Even though I may soon be a model, I still have to deal with the real me.

But I do like how, when the classes are over, I'll automatically become a model in the agency. I know that doesn't guarantee that I'll be a success, but at least I've got a shot at it. Modeling still seems like more fun than a lot of my life has been up to this point.

And sometimes having the people at the school tell me I'm pretty fills a space in my heart that I thought was destroyed forever—the space that got taken over by all my sadness.

Bashiyrah was 15 when she wrote this story.

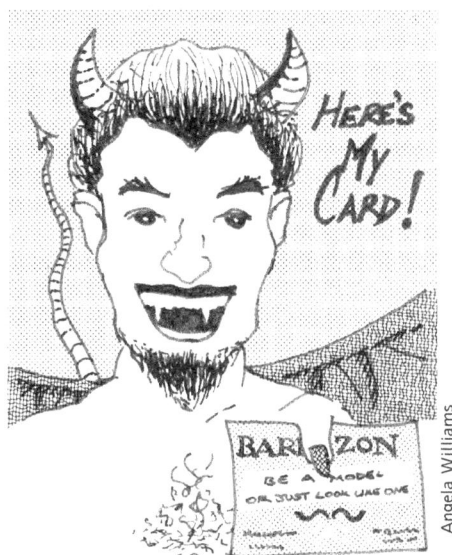

Angela Williams

I Was a Beauty School Sucker

By Tonya Leslie

A few years ago as I was looking through a magazine, a headline loomed in my face: "Be a Model or Just Look Like One. Barbizon Can Show You How."

I was ecstatic! How often had I dreamed of having my face on a magazine cover, of being sought after by the press and loved by the public. (That's a little much, but you get the idea.)

I begged my parents to let me go to Barbizon. After all, how many times had I endured piano lessons and Girl Scouts, the things they wanted me to do? I had finally found something I wanted and the least they could do was finance it, right?

Right!

So we went for our initial visit to the Barbizon office in Queens, New York. Upon looking at me, the woman in charge predicted my success as a model. They even sweet-talked my sister into joining as a kind of two-for-one deal.

After a few weeks of training, the woman said, my modeling success was practically guaranteed. The parents, too, were so convinced that they didn't grumble about the $1,000-plus they kicked out. I guess they assumed we would make it all back.

At the first session, my sister and I were outfitted with our modeling essentials: a handbook and a makeup brush kit. We had three hour-long classes every Saturday. They included make-up training, exercise class, and runway modeling.

The makeup classes were more like makeup disaster classes. Rather than telling us how to apply makeup according to our skin color (we're black) and the shape of our faces, they gave a general analysis. In other words, we all put on the same makeup, the same way. What happened to the natural beauty of youth? Well, that's not the way at Barbizon—they seemed to emphasize the more makeup, the better.

Fully loaded with makeup, we went on to runway modeling where we modeled imaginary clothing. You know, fur coats and other clothing, the likes of which we would never see. We were taught something called a model stance and shown how to go up and down steps.

Then we did group modeling, where we would pair off and make poses. I'd never seen runway shows like this, but I figured the teachers at Barbizon knew the deal better than I did. That was my first and constant mistake.

Weeks passed and graduation approached. We grew bored with the classes so we skipped a few—well, more than a few. Then we weren't really prepared for graduation, so we decided to make up classes.

That was difficult because Barbizon classes go in no specific order. For example, on a Saturday you may take class number four without ever taking class number three. My sister and I ended up taking several classes over and over again. Not fun at all.

Finally, a year after we began, graduation was around the corner. A photographer was called in to take shots of the girls. This was to be very professional, so a makeup artist and hairstylist were called in, too, although they were supposedly optional.

My sister and I wanted to do our own makeup and hair. We figured we knew what looked good, or at least we should after all this time and money, but my teacher assured me that their people were the very best. Then she commented that our hair and makeup hardly looked professional.

Recovering from that insult, we handed over the additional $35 each, figuring, once again, that the teachers knew best. Big mistake number two. After posing in a variety of outfits and makeup styles, I glanced in the mirror. My makeup and hair looked like something out of Barbizon Hell.

I figured the teachers at Barbizon knew the deal better than I did. That was my first mistake.

First of all, my medium-toned skin, with the help of tons of foundation, was at least four tones darker. (Not to mention the lovely lines where my foundation and skin color didn't match.) Then they showered me with frosted pink blush and lipstick, completing the look with baby blue eye-shadow. Those colors may work for Barbie, but not for me.

And then my hair. Let's just say that relaxed black hair should not be teased five feet and then sprayed with a can of hair spray. (Unless you like the, tangled, dry, split end—let's not forget flaky—look that will follow in the morning.)

Upon viewing my stricken looks, the teacher told me that retouching and recoloring on photos is common (in my case, mandatory) and the pictures would look great. Like a fool, I believed her, adding mistake number three. (Surely you're counting along, right?)

A couple of weeks later, the pictures were delivered to my house. Not only did we look bad (I would describe my sister's pictures, but she promised instant death at the mere mention), we felt bad. We felt bad because of the screaming fit the parents threw once they saw those ugly $300 pictures.

Well, we didn't go to graduation after that little scene. In fact, we never went back. The pictures are still in the back of my sister's closet...somewhere. Our parents make us take the pictures out every once in a while when I wonder aloud why they don't raise my allowance or why we never get gifts or have parties.

One day on the train, a guy approached me and said, "You look like a model," then he handed me his card. I ripped it to pieces in his face. I'm sure I don't have to tell you what company he was from.

Tonya was 18 when she wrote this story. She works in publishing and is co-author of the book True You, recommended by Oprah as a resource for mothers and daughters.

Stephanie Wilson

Beauty or Beast?

By Angelina Darrisaw

"Sometimes I shave my legs and sometimes I don't," sings India. Arie in her song "Video." "It really just depends on whatever feels good in my soul." I can definitely relate.

I do shave often in the summer for the hot weather's shorts and sleeveless clothing, but sometimes I question why. Constant shaving can lead to razor bumps, burns, ingrown hairs, dark spots and other problems that look worse than a little bush. Shaving can also be annoying, but it's a part of the price we women pay to be pretty.

The first time I shaved, I was on vacation in the summer after 4th grade. My older cousin and I decided we were too hairy and got a hold of one of my mother's razors. We shaved each other's legs and afterwards they felt so smooth and good.

Little did we know that once you start, you can't stop—not if you want your legs to stay smooth. The stubble of hair grew back rough over the next few days and we did it again. But after we went back home, we both stopped.

I started up again in 7th grade. I'd gone to coed school until then, but when I started going to an all-girls school, the girls told me hairy bodies were a no-no. I begged my mom to buy me a pink Gillette razor. She didn't think I should start shaving so early, but I told her, "Look at how hairy I am!"

She gave in, and I shaved often after that. I experimented with creams and hair removers, but I went back to shaving because it was easier and it didn't smell bad. And I love the baby soft skin that I get as a result.

But when I wake up some days, I don't care how natural I look or how stubbly I am. I've gone outside wearing sleeveless shirts with dark hair under my arms. And I like it.

I've gone outside wearing sleeveless shirts with dark hair under my arms. And I like it.

My mother will say something like, "You look very natural." My friends are more direct. They'll just tell me, "You forgot to shave." My mom is right, though; it is completely natural. It's just hair, right? What's the big deal? I don't understand why body hair is such a turn off.

A lot of men seem to find women with legs and underarms that mirror their own unattractive. One man told me he wouldn't even date a woman if she had a moderate underarm bush. He said it's part of being beautiful, and a woman would have to realize that if she didn't shave, she would get approached less.

And a friend of mine told me that underarm hair is nasty because it shows a girl has bad hygiene. Since when is shaving part of being clean? You can bathe twice a day and get every nook and cranny, but still not feel like shaving. Having hair doesn't make me or anyone else any less clean.

Most guys don't shave there, so why should I? I realize that shaving is like putting on makeup. The idea is that we are enhancing our features by shaving. But even more, it's also about conforming to the societal belief that women's body hair—when it's not piled on their heads—is unattractive.

It takes the same kind of confidence for a woman in today's judgmental society to have a hairy body as it does for her to have a bald head. A woman who doesn't feel the need to shave is confident enough in her beauty that she doesn't need to conform. That's a confidence I respect.

But it's not a confidence I share. When it comes to shaving, I conform like everyone else. In the winter, I slack off and shave very little, since no one will notice. But for right now, I think I'll go with the weather. As long as the summer season lasts, I'll appreciate the smooth, groomed feel of my underarms and legs just after shaving.

Angelina was 15 when she wrote this story. She later graduated from Davidson College in North Carolina.

Maurice Anderson

Trying Femininity on for Size

By Debbie Seraphin

Growing up, I was always around boys. I have two older brothers and we have always been very close. So what they did, I did. What they wore, I wore. I climbed gates and walls, rode bikes, and played every type of sport. I dressed in baggy jeans, T-shirts, and sneakers. I had no idea what feminine was. The fellas thought it was cool having me around, so I just enjoyed myself, not realizing how all of this was going to affect me later on in my life.

In elementary school, I thought being a tomboy was cool. I didn't stand out that much because everybody dressed like a tomboy back then. The baggy style and hat-to-the-back look were in. The way of dress was very similar for both girls and boys.

When I was around 9, I noticed that other girls weren't like me. They were playing with dolls and having tea parties, things I was not allowed to do. My parents said that playing those games was like preparing to have a baby and a husband and that I was too young to have those ideas in my head. Since I knew my parents wouldn't allow it, I never let myself get too interested in dolls or dress up or other girls' games. I just wanted to know why other girls liked them so much.

To be honest, I wasn't much interested in sports either. What I did enjoy was reading, dancing, and singing. I could do those things by myself and still have a good time. But since my brothers were always playing sports and my parents made me go everywhere with them, I had no choice.

Still, I was basically happy with who I was until I arrived in junior high school. That was a period of hell. The kids would call me a tomboy because I wore baggy jeans, sweatshirts, and braids in my hair. To make things worse, I was taller and skinnier than all the rest of the girls and I was underdeveloped. The other kids would hit me in my chest and say that they couldn't be hurting me, because I had nothing there. They would say, "Hurry up and grow. Then we won't have to hit you anymore."

One time in art class, a boy came up to me and started dissing on me for the entire period. He said, "Why do you look like you have no chest and no body? All you do is wear those dodo braids in your hair. You are so skinny and ugly. You are never going to change because you are naturally a chickenhead." I cried for the entire period while the rest of the class laughed at me. I was so embarrassed.

I believed everything everyone told me to hurt my feelings. I thought I did not deserve to live. I went home crying every day because I did not like myself. I felt like an ugly duckling. In addition to my flat chest, I had skinny legs and knobby knees. I was always asking myself, "Why do I have to look like this, and when am I going to change?"

All of my close friends were already dating. They were pretty and smart and had everything going for them. When they were with their boyfriends, I felt left out. I never told them how I felt because I thought if I opened up, they would just mock me.

When prom night came in the 8th grade, I was determined to prove to myself that I could fit in. This was going to be my big breakthrough. My mom and I went shopping for a new dress and shoes. I wore an elegant purple gown with rhinestones at the straps and black slingback high-heeled pumps. My hair was done in drop curls with a bang in the front. This was the first time I had ever tried to be feminine, my big transformation.

When I first walked in, I was nervous because I didn't know how everyone was going to react to me. But I felt good in my dress and enjoyed the attention I was getting. My friends were surprised at how nice I looked and heads actually turned. Everyone was wondering who the new girl was. I was having a good time. Then, just when I was thinking, "I did it," something had to go wrong.

I was always asking myself, "Why do I have to look like this, and when am I going to change?"

I was going into the girls' bathroom and a guy walked past and said, "Shouldn't you be going to the boys' bathroom with me? Because you surely look like a boy to me, Shorty."

Boy, was I pissed! I wanted to curse him out but I didn't have the courage. I went home and cried instead. I had thought this was going to be my night. After all, this was my prom night. But, no! I had to get hurt and be brought down from my one good day in that school.

I decided that when I got to high school, I was going to change. Not just in terms of the way I looked, like I did for the prom. But in terms of how I acted. I wanted to stop being so shy and easily intimidated.

When I went to school on the first day of my freshman year, I decided to study the other girls to get ideas for the new me. I watched the way they talked, dressed, and acted. I saw the older girls always making sure that they were heard, being very sassy with teachers and flirting with the guys in a friendly way. And they were all popular.

I thought there was only one way to be feminine and this was it. I didn't know anything else. So I just picked up on what I saw and copied it, even though it wasn't me. I said to myself, "If I act like they do, I might get the same reaction."

I t worked. I became loud, talkative, and rude. I developed a sassy attitude and everyone seemed to like it. I decided to change my appearance too. I processed my hair and started wearing it in various styles that everyone enjoyed. And, day by day, I added something different to my wardrobe.

I started wearing nice small blouses instead of T-shirts, fitted jeans instead of baggy ones, and shoes instead of sneakers. People started to notice that my style was changing for the better. My transformation was going so well that I went a little overboard. My parents had always been very strict with me, especially in terms of how I dressed. No revealing clothing was allowed. But at this point in my life, I wanted attention and all eyes on me.

During my junior and senior years, I decided to rebel against my parents. I went from the nice small blouses to short belly tops, from fitted jeans to tight jeans or short skirts, and from shoes to high-heeled hooker boots. My parents went crazy, of course, but dressing like that made me feel positive about myself.

I rebelled in other ways too. My parents were so busy trying to protect me from bad influences that they had never let me sleep over at other people's houses, or go hang out with my friends, or even go to the movies. I was such a goody two-shoes all my life; now it was time for me to spread my wings. I started to stay out late, travel around the city, and go over to my friends' houses.

My parents yelled at me, talked to my teachers, called my

friends, invaded my privacy and spied on me. It didn't work, because I was still sneaky in my own small ways. Then they gave up, deciding that I had to learn my own lesson.

At first, I was having such a good time that I didn't pay my parents any mind. Then, during my senior year, I saw the pain I was putting them through and stopped all the running around. I decided to balance my wild side with my old, calmer side.

Now I go out once in a while, but mostly I am busy getting through my first year of college, being an active member of my church, job-hunting, and writing in my spare time. It's taken a long time, but I am finally happy with myself and my self-esteem is over the roof. I no longer worry about fitting in and being liked. I talk to all types of people and go to all types of places and feel accepted and respected. I love to wake up every morning and look at myself in the mirror, because I feel beautiful inside and out. I'm finally being myself and being feminine at the same time.

Now I realize that there are many different ways of acting feminine.

I never got to be myself until now. My identity always came from everybody else. When I was younger, I was a tomboy because that's what my family wanted me to be. In junior high, I wanted to be seen as feminine, like the other girls, but I didn't know how to change. In high school, I thought there was only one way to be feminine—the rude, sarcastic, flirtatious style the other girls had. I copied their style and I finally fit in, but it still wasn't me.

Now I realize that there are many different ways of acting feminine. There's the classy, sassy, sarcastic way, and there's the polite, respectful, calm-hearted way. Another way is a mixture of both. That's my way. Who I am now and what I look like now make everything I had to go through to get here worth it. So I thank all those fellas who put me through all that persecution in junior high. All of you have made me a better person.

To anyone who is now going through what I went through back then, I say: "It's going to be OK. You will survive." And to the guys who used to hit me in the chest and make fun of me for being undeveloped, I just want you to know: "You cannot hit me anymore, because if you did, you would get the biggest beatdown of your life."

Debbie was 17 when she wrote this story. She attended Bronx Community College and cosmetology school.

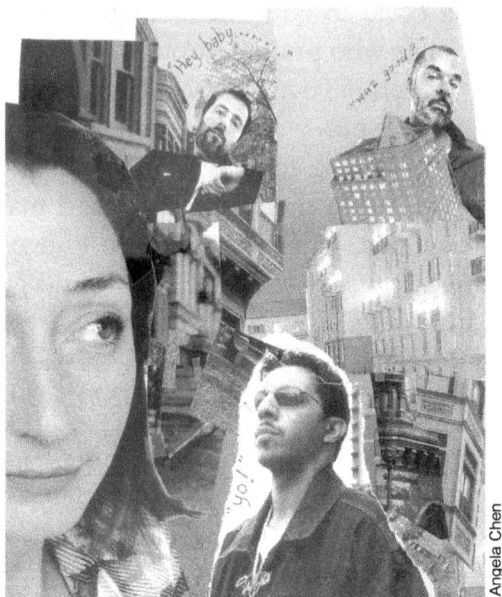

Angela Chen

Covering My Butt

By LaToya Souvenir

I can't remember a time in my life when I didn't feel self-conscious about my body. In elementary school it seemed my uniform was the only one that rose up high in the back. In junior high, I often heard guys yell out, "Look at that girl's big butt!" on my way to class.

I already knew that I was well-endowed in the rear area—I didn't need to be reminded every few minutes. Didn't the other kids realize how much their comments hurt? All I wanted to do was to fit in. After school I would come home and cry myself to sleep.

In high school, the guys got bolder and the comments got more perverted. I must have heard every "fat butt" line in the book walking down those hallways. Like I didn't already know. Didn't they understand that it was my body? I had to live with it every day of my life.

One day at the beginning of my sophomore year, I was on my way home from school and, when the subway made a stop, a bunch of guys about my age got on. I was standing close to the door holding onto the pole, when I noticed that several of them were looking me up and down, the way you look at a new coat before you buy it. I began to feel very uncomfortable and moved to the other end of the car. They just kept right on staring.

Then they started talking about me as if I wasn't there, saying things like, "Yo, look at the butt on her," and "Damn I want me some of that." I stood there wishing the floor would open up and swallow me right there. The other passengers in the car started looking at me really funny and the comments kept on coming.

When I finally got to my stop, one of them had the nerve to block my way and ask me if I would give him my number. I just rolled my eyes, said, "Excuse me," and stepped off the train. That day I came to the conclusion that I had to do something. I was tired of all the lewd comments. My dreaded rear end had to be hidden from the rest of the world. I decided my only escape was to wear oversized clothes.

I started buying jeans with a 34 waist instead of my usual 28, and extra large T-shirts (I couldn't wear my usual T-shirts with baggy pants). Dressing like that made me feel so uncomfortable, but I did it anyway to escape the comments. Still, I missed clothes that fit. I missed my cute dresses and shoes to match. In their place I now wore $80 sneakers that were draining my pockets dry.

Although the expense was sometimes a little too much to handle, the clothing did have the desired effect. The comments didn't stop completely, but they were a lot less frequent and almost never about my behind.

I had been thinking of becoming a cheerleader or running track. But I decided not to because I was afraid of what people would say if they saw me in one of those little uniforms. I told a friend about my decision. She was a super senior and a cheer-leader and I looked up to her. People were always talking about how rude she was, how she thought she was all that, and how fat she was, but she never let any of it bother her.

When I explained to her why I hadn't tried out for any of the teams, she was upset. "Who the hell cares what people have to say about you?" she said. "People are going to always talk no matter what you do. Damn Toya, I can't believe you let that change your mind."

That Saturday, I threw all caution to the wind and bought a skirt.

That (and the fact that neither my parents nor my pockets could afford it anymore) was the push I needed to be able to ignore those comments that made me feel disgusting. That Saturday, I threw all caution to the wind and bought a skirt.

At first, I was a little afraid of going back to my old way of dressing. I had grown accustomed to the luxury of walking down the street in peace. But I decided to hell with it, I was not going to let some nasty men who had never learned the right way to speak to women run my life.

When I went back to school after summer vacation, my friends were shocked. "You're dressing like a girl again," they exclaimed. Not only that but I also felt good about myself for a change.

Since then, guys have said some really perverted things, but I just ignore them. I've learned not to let it bother me so much, and if it does I speak up. When a guy says something really disgusting that makes me angry, I usually let him know how I feel, or I insult him in front of the same people he is trying to impress. What my friend said is true: people are always going to talk, no matter what you do or what you look like.

LaToya was 17 when she wrote this story. She later graduated from college with a degree in public administration.

Catalina Buitrago

Naturally Thin

By Desirée Guéry

When I walk into a room, it feels like everyone looks at me. No, I'm not a super model. I'm just a normal teenage Latina with brown eyes and straight brown hair. I usually wear comfortable clothing, like blue jeans and T-shirts. Nothing fancy, nothing racy.

But at 5'6" and 105 lbs, I am thinner than the "average" girl, wearing size small shirts and size 3 jeans and skirts. I was called a "stick figure" in elementary school because of my thin arms and legs.

And now, years later, I can't count the times that people have gasped when they saw me, and then whispered to the person beside them, "She's so skinny!"

Those are the polite ones. Some people feel the need to shout it out. After I turned 14, I started to get the infamously rude "cat calls" from guys on the street, who said things like, "You're skinny, but that's OK! Sexy anyway."

And I had to deal with one particularly humiliating moment last winter, as a new student in my high school. As soon as I walked into my English class, two girls I didn't know—I'll call them Laura and Mary—ceased their conversation to stare at me.

"Oh my God!" Laura said, causing everyone to stare in our direction. "You are so skinny! I mean, look at you! You're skin and bones!"

It felt like she was being so loud that even people in another state could hear her. I couldn't tell if she meant it as a compliment or an insult.

"That's mean," Mary told her.

I knew other classmates were staring, so I took my seat in front of them and sat down quietly, mustering up a smile, not saying anything. I thought maybe if I ignored her, she'd shut up.

"It's not mean. It's the truth!" said Laura. "Come on now. Have you even eaten this year?" She continued on and on until I turned around and said, "Just because I'm 20 lbs skinnier than you doesn't mean you have the right to announce it to the world. There are plenty of things I could say about your weight."

"Oooh," said our fellow classmates. After a moment of silence, Laura said, "God, you don't have to be so rude about it." She was the one being rude, but I just left it at that.

People's comments have made me feel self-conscious about my weight. Because it's fashionable to be thin, I know that some people point out my weight as a compliment, which feels good to hear. But when people make a big deal about how skinny I am, it makes me feel like an object. Each time they stare, I feel low, like an outcast.

I hadn't noticed that I was thinner than most others until I went to elementary school, where I realized I was the skinniest one in my class. My kindergarten teacher even gave me extra snacks. I didn't know it was an attempt to fatten me up. I just assumed I was special.

My grandmother and mother used to give me food all the

time as well. I ate and ate and ate, asked for more because I was still hungry, ate some more, but always stayed the same weight. I have a high metabolism, which means I burn calories quickly. So to this day, no matter how much I eat, I don't gain weight.

Being thin isn't that common in my family. The only two relatives I know who're skinny are my uncle Eddie and my grandmother. Everyone else is either "normal" or slightly chubby, which makes me stand out.

So family members usually try to fatten me up at holiday dinners. Even though they know I'm naturally thin, it doesn't stop them from hitting me with a round of questions if I don't finish my plate.

I often stare at myself in the mirror, trying to find what's so weird about me.

"Do you feel sick?" "Are you full already?" "Do you want something else to eat?" I prefer to suck it up and eat rather than be interrogated for not eating.

To make matters worse, some people who don't know me well wonder if I'm bulimic or anorexic. I've had doctors ask me about my eating habits, fearful that I was starving myself. Friends joke about me having an eating disorder (although I don't laugh), and strangers insinuate it with their looks of pity.

It hurts, because I can't believe people could automatically assume that about me. Why can't I be naturally thin without starving myself? I can't change, and I wish people didn't make me feel like I have to.

I often go home and stare at myself in the mirror, trying to find what's so weird about me. I don't see myself as being extremely skinny, but after all the stares and random comments from people on the street, I question myself as I stare. "What would make me acceptable? Should I wear baggy clothes so that I look bigger?" I wonder.

At times, I wear baggier outfits that make me look like I weigh more, even though loose clothes make me feel uncomfortable because they feel as if they're going to fall off.

Sometimes I ask myself, "If I were prettier, would people still gawk at me? If they did, would they mean it in a nicer way?" So I try to make myself more attractive by wearing more makeup or trendier clothes.

But other times I don't care what anyone thinks of my weight. I hear the same comments so often that they sometimes bounce off me as if I'm immune to them.

I still usually wear fitted clothes, because it makes me feel like myself. And I try to focus on the positive comments from my family and friends. Some of my friends tell me I'm so lucky to be as thin as I am, especially because I can eat as much as I do without gaining weight.

If I'm out to eat with my friends and I order dessert, they'll say something like, "Oh, I can't order anything. I'm too fat for that."

But they're not fat, they're just not as thin as me. Either way, they're perfect the way they are. It's silly that they won't eat a slice of cake or an ice cream cone once in a while. I feel lucky that I can enjoy eating whatever I want.

When people make a big deal about how skinny I am, it makes me feel like an object.

Plus, I can always squeeze into seats when there's hardly any room. If I drop something in a small space, I can always get it. There are plenty of great things about being thin.

But as I struggle to become comfortable with my weight, someone's comments always get me down again. I went to the pizzeria for lunch a few days ago to get a slice of baked ziti pizza. As the man behind the counter got my slice, he looked back and forth from the slice to me.

"You sure you can eat this? Maybe you should get a plain slice," he said. "It's smaller."

"Why wouldn't I be able to eat it?" I asked, trying not to get upset.

"Well, you're a small girl. You might not eat it all."

"I know what I want," I replied. "And if you don't want to serve it to me, I can go elsewhere."

With that note, he put the slice in the oven. Incidents like this make me wonder if I'll ever be completely comfortable with my weight. But they won't stop me from trying.

Desirée was 16 when she wrote this story.

Carolina Moya

Mirror, Mirror on the Wall

By I. Okolo

Often when we search in the mirror, we are looking for something beyond our reflection. Maybe it is our soul we're looking for, or our strength we're trying to gain. Maybe we're trying to discover who we really are or want to be. I call it looking for our true beauty.

But as we search for our true beauty, we don't always know how to find it or even understand what we're searching for. Sometimes the search can overwhelm us with depression. We stare at the mirror focusing more on what we dislike about how we look than on discovering who we are. We become obsessed with our appearance.

That's the process I went through when I was 13. Those days I let my soul be fooled into thinking that true beauty was all about being skinny, and having the perfect hair, eyes, and face. I also thought true beauty was having the complexion of my mother, a light-skinned woman.

At that age, I had pimples all over my face and was heavy-set. My hair was very damaged. I just felt ugly. I've ripped up almost all the pictures of me from that time because I felt so negative about myself. I think that if I saw one, even now, I would start focusing on what was wrong with how I looked in that picture rather than who I am today.

My family made it even harder for me. Often my mother would say, "No man will ever marry you because you are so ugly." She'd say that I didn't look anything like a girl. My brothers always called me ugly to the point of death. They wouldn't even be seen in public with me.

One time I got into an argument with my sister and she told me that when I was a baby, my mother gave me away to her sister for two years because I was so ugly. My mother said she did it for other reasons, but I never knew who to believe.

There were many painful things that happened to me in my childhood besides feeling ugly: There was rape and sexual abuse, physical and mental abuse, emotional abuse and drug and alcohol abuse. Plus, from being hit so much, I lost my hearing. All these things made me feel so hopeless. And I took all the hate that had been heaped on me and learned how to hate myself. What I focused on was hating my appearance.

I thought that if I were beautiful, I would be free from worry.

I thought that if I were beautiful, I would be free from worry, free from depression, and I would have the finer things in life (men, money, jewels, and happiness). So I had to do whatever I could to make myself look better.

When I was about 14, I began my beauty routine. I used bleaching cream to make my face lighter. You were supposed to mix one cream with another because the first cream was so strong. But I wanted to be light so badly that I used the first cream straight. In just about a week there was an amazing difference. Despite this, I continued to use it because I wanted to become even lighter.

But after about three weeks, I looked like I had a black body and a white face. Everyone started to make fun of me. It got so bad that I stopped going to school. I couldn't bear to show my face to the world any longer.

I didn't go back to school for two whole years. Instead, I stayed upstairs on the third floor of my apartment building reading books or just sitting. When school was over, I would walk downstairs, ring the bell of my house, and act like I had just come back from school.

I continued to try to change whatever people disliked about me. I used hair dyes to gain back a little of my complexion and bleach to bleach the spots that had stayed very dark. I periodically starved myself to be skinny. I would go to school with less than a dollar so I couldn't buy a lot of food.

All my efforts didn't help. I started breaking out even more, gaining weight and, worst of all, losing control of my inner self. I found myself growing more and more depressed.

I felt so ugly that I thought I would never get a date or even have a friend. I felt so lonely. My soul became friendly with death. I even tried to commit suicide.

The mirror became my worst enemy. The way I looked in it made me feel like dying. Even when I didn't look in the mirror, I felt like I could see how ugly I was in other people's eyes. It was as if the whole world was a mirror showing me my disgrace.

I went to live in a foster care group home when I was 15, but nothing got better. During my first two years in the group home, almost every day someone would tell me, "You are so ugly," or ask me, "Why are you ugly?" Many days I would lie in my room crying, praying, and writing out all my pain in my diary.

In the group home, I became bulimic. After a while I could hardly eat without throwing up. Every time I threw up I told myself that it would be my last time. But watching the food come out felt like a release. It felt as if I were crying. In truth, it was more like bleeding.

Then one day we were having a meeting at my cottage and one of the staff said, "If we were to make ourselves then we would make ourselves with long hair and beautiful eyes and a slim body, but since God made us, we have to accept ourselves as we are."

I might have been told to accept myself before, but this time there was something in the staff's tone that was able to awaken me. Maybe it was the fact that even though she didn't have the face or body of a model, the way she carried herself made her a beautiful woman. She had that power. She was a woman of her words.

I looked at her and I just felt like, "Phew." I felt like that was the most beautiful and touching gift I had ever received. I suddenly felt my mind open. I started questioning all the things I'd been doing.

I realized that if I accepted that God was perfect, that meant that I needed to accept how He had made me. I began to challenge myself to accept how I was and believe in me.

Not everything changed after that. I continued to diet and try to improve my appearance. I continued to feel depressed because my mother's voice kept

It wasn't easy, but I fought every day to believe in myself.

on overwhelming my soul. Those things she used to say to me, like, "No man will ever marry you because you are too ugly," I couldn't get fully out of my head.

But I also started to say in my prayers, "God, I know I am beautiful." And usually I thanked Him for making me the way I am.

I decided that I would not allow myself to be emotionally abused ever again. I gave myself the name "Queen of Africa," and I walked around with the attitude of a queen. I began to dress in creative styles, and I got a tattoo of a rose on my chest to show that I, and no one else, had control over my body (although I hid it from staff for many years, because I was afraid of what they would think).

Over time I began to see things in me that others were not able to see, like my beautiful smile, my beautiful eyes. I began to appreciate the poet in me and enjoy my own sense of style. Before, I was blind to those things. Removing the veil wasn't an easy process, but I fought every day to believe in myself.

Some girls mocked me for my new attitude. They called me all kinds of names, which hurt. But I ignored them. I tried to inhale gratitude for just being.

By the time I was 19, I felt and looked better. Around that time, many things about my appearance improved. I was no longer breaking out as much as I used to. My weight went down. My creative style expressed who I was and where I was coming from.

I think part of it was that I was happier, and my body let those new feelings of joy shine through. Some of it was negative. After all, I was still bulimic. Bulimia was the fear in me that if I ate, I'd go back to the way I used to be when people didn't like me. Even though I felt better about myself, it was very hard to stop.

Still, a lot of guys started to tell me that I was beautiful, in my eyes, my smile, and my style. I felt exhilarated because my hard work had paid off.

I'd like to say that all I needed to do was find my inner beauty, but it really did help that my outer appearance had improved, too. As children we're told that beauty is on the inside. But we all worry about our appearance. And when we look better, people react to us more positively, and we feel better about ourselves.

But improving my appearance didn't make everything perfect, the way I once thought it would. To be beautiful is one thing, but to feel beautiful is another. That was something I had to learn.

It's true that on many more days than in my past, I feel positive about myself. I don't compare myself to others nearly as much and I'm more confident, too. But often, I am still depressed, and on those days, it can be hard not to feel ugly.

When I feel alone and really need to be wanted, I still look in the mirror and wonder what's wrong with me that makes me so unwanted. I look in that mirror and begin to say, "If I could only change this, if I could only change that." Sometimes I think my eyes will never be satisfied with what they see.

On days when I feel really bad, I still throw up my food. I used to do it three times a day, and now I only do it once every few weeks. That's better. But I want to stop completely. I ask myself, "Why do I do the things I do?" I think that answering that question will help me stop.

When I began to ask myself why looking better didn't make me perfectly happy, when that was all I ever thought I wanted, I realized that what I had achieved was not the point of life. It's the struggle behind that achievement that is really the point.

I've begun to understand that trying to feel good about myself is a lifetime's work. I no longer need to tell myself that I'm a queen, but I try to express it in how I walk and dress, and in my poetry. And I struggle to accept myself, because I know that feeling good is about getting to know who I am, and being OK with that. I know much better than I knew before that beauty without happiness is like a sound without a voice—empty.

The author was 21 when she wrote this story. She has since graduated from college with a business degree.

Jamaal Pascall

Beauty Is More Than Skin Deep

By Danielle Wilson

My friends always ask me, "Why are you always looking in the mirror?" or "Why are you so confident about yourself?" I know it might be hard to believe, but until the age of 14, I never really thought of myself as beautiful or ugly. I thought of myself as an average person.

When I was 12, I never really cared about how I looked. I was a short, skinny girl with a couple of ponytails (because my grandmother used to do my hair all the time) and thousands of bumps on my face.

In my 6th grade class, one boy used to call me "bumpy road" or "mountain." Yeah, it used to get to me. In fact, it got to me so much that I knocked him right out of his chair. I know that was mean, but he was being mean to me!

And guess what? He saw me recently and he now wants to know when I'm going to be his girl. Please! I wouldn't give him the time of day because he hasn't changed. But I certainly have.

During the summer I turned 14, I started recognizing my beauty a little more. I started by taking care of my face, washing it more and going to the dermatologist for my acne.

Of course, boys started to notice me. I've always had a perfect shape and never had a problem with my weight. I also changed the way I dressed. I started to show off my figure by wearing skirts and jeans that really fit. I also started doing my own hair. I can't really remember how I did it, but my grandmother used to say, "Lord, you come up with the weirdest hairstyles. Just like your mother when she was little."

That was the best summer of my life because I was getting mad compliments from the cutest boys. Whenever they complimented me I would say, "I know!" because I knew I looked good. Didn't I?

I became stuck-up because I was getting compliments like crazy and I wasn't used to this kind of attention. Before I turned 14, I don't think anybody ever noticed me. Now that I had blossomed like a flower, I wanted the whole world to know.

You can say I got gassed because every time I passed a car window, I stared at my reflection and sang to myself that I was the most beautiful-est thing in the world.

When I was younger, I never looked in mirrors because I didn't like what I saw. Meaning, a face full of pimples. Now mirrors became my life. My attitude got so bad that I used to tell boys, "I'm too pretty to be with you," or "Don't touch me."

One day about two years ago, I went with my friend to her boyfriend's house. There was a boy there who wanted to meet me, and he was not what I expected. In fact, I thought he was ugly. He had little beady eyes and big lips. He sort of scared me.

The first time I looked at him, I yelled "No!" really loud. Then I turned to my friend and yelled, "He is so damn ugly. What's wrong with you? Why did you try to play me and hook me up with this thing?" I thought I looked so good I couldn't stand to be around anyone ugly.

After he heard that, he left. I guess he was mad. Then my friend's boyfriend said that I was wrong. I said, "I can't help it if your friend is ugly. You know, you shouldn't hang out with ugly people because they make you look bad." After that, a friend picked me up and I left.

Another time, a boy tried to talk to me when my friends and I were coming from a party. And I ran from him, because I didn't like the shape of his head. His head was little on a big body. He looked like a cartoon and he had scars and pimples all over his face. My friends never forgot that. They still tease me about it to this day.

I used to tell boys to their faces that they were ugly and that I looked too good to be with them. And they would just stand there and take what I said. None of them ever cursed me out or raised their hands to me. But then one day, when I was about 15, a boy named Rick turned my whole attitude around.

Rick and I were sitting in the park and we were arguing. He was never my man, but we were friends leading to that. We had met at a party, but his friend liked me.

I got mad at something I can't quite remember, and I said, "I'm too pretty to be with you or your friend."

Rick said, "You're right, but with that attitude you will be by yourself. You could be as pretty as you wanna be to a boy, but if you have a bad attitude they won't want anything to do with you. They will do nothing but use you." And then he walked away.

Right then and there I wanted to run up to him and curse him out because I couldn't believe what he had said to me. I was furious! I was so furious that I couldn't wait until I got home so I could call him to curse him out.

But when I got home, I was too mad to do it. And besides, I knew that he was going to call me to apologize. But I was wrong. Rick never called me back.

I thought about what Rick said and about all the times I had told boys I was too pretty for them. I started to realize that I had let my looks take over my inner person. I didn't even remember how I used to be. My stuck-up attitude had become my whole personality. And I told myself that I was going to change.

Changing wasn't easy—there were times when I wanted to tell a boy that I was too pretty for him. But I held back.

The reason why Rick had such a big impact on me was because he was the first and only boy who wouldn't let me talk to him like that. He stood up to me, and I'm glad he did before my attitude got worse.

I told boys they were ugly and that I looked too good to be with them.

I still look in the mirror for hours and look into car windows, checking out my reflection. There's nothing wrong with that. You don't have to be stuck-up just because you admire yourself. But after Rick said that to me, I started to be nice to boys. I accepted compliments in a nicer way by saying, "Thank you," every time someone said I was pretty, instead of saying, "I know."

I also started paying more attention to my interests, like writing and reading, instead of my looks. I wrote short stories for contests in my school, and I won second place. As I improved my writing, I finally won first place. I was so happy!

I did more than help myself. I helped someone else—my friend Tasha. Tasha wasn't stuck-up like me. She was miserable all the time because she thought she was ugly. She used to always ask me, "How do you get your hair like that?" So one day I told her that I was going to do her hair.

After I did her hair, she was still a little doubtful about her looks because she didn't like the way she dressed. So I took Tasha shopping. (Not with my money, her money. I didn't become that nice.) And we had a blast. I didn't tell her what to pick out. It was her choice. But she asked me for advice and fashion tips.

After we finished, Tasha said she felt great and that she never had so much fun in her life. She also said she owed it all to me. Then I told her, "It wasn't me who changed you. You changed you. Now, don't change your attitude because you changed your looks. Stay the nice person you are."

If it wasn't for Rick, I wouldn't have done this for Tasha. I probably would have thought that Tasha just wanted to be like me or something. What I learned was this: To be beautiful, it has to be more inside than out.

So, if you're someone like me, take my advice: Looks ain't everything, sister! I had to learn the hard way. But if you're someone who isn't hung up on your looks, before you make that big step to improve yourself—don't change your attitude.

Danielle was 16 when she wrote this story.

Christina Pacheco

I Took Dieting Too Far

By Renu George

When I was really little, I was thin and I could tell that was a good thing to be. I was praised for my picky eating habits, while my chubby cousin was reprimanded for putting an extra helping of rice on her plate. My parents used up rolls of film just on me. I would always pose and smile a toothy grin, which led my relatives to predict a future career in modeling for me.

I was 7 years old when I began to gain weight. I spent the summer in India with my grandmother, who wouldn't stop feeding me Indian sweets and curries. I came back to America with a sweet tooth and a lot of clothes that no longer fit me.

My parents chided me softly, saying that I was beginning to look like my fat cousin. I began sneaking cups of ice cream from the kitchen to my bedroom, so that I wouldn't have to see the disappointment in their eyes when I ate. The boasts about my finicky eating stopped. My father started calling me "rolly-poly" and wouldn't let me wear shorts outside in the company of his friends.

By the time I was 8, I was totally self-conscious about my weight. One day, while my 3rd grade teacher was reading to us, I stared at the sight of my thighs spread out over my chair. They seemed so huge to me, oozing out in every direction. While the other kids sat at the edge of their seats, wondering what would happen next, I was drawing pictures in my mind of how fat I must look in my little yellow sweatpants—like a tub of butter.

In 5th grade, I learned that the old children's rhyme, "Sticks and stones may break my bones, but words will never hurt me," was one of the biggest lies ever spoken. Whenever we had a fight, my friends would make mooing sounds, or pretend the floor was shaking when I walked by. We would always hug and make up the next day, but part of me felt that if I weren't fat, no one would make fun of me anymore.

Losing weight became like a game. I wanted to see how many pounds I could lose and how fast.

Things got worse when I entered middle school. I started to read the teen magazines that told you how girls were supposed to look. My thoughts also began to turn from hopscotch and jump rope to guys. I noticed that they smiled more appreciatively at the skinny little girls than at me. Whenever I passed by mirrors, windows, or any shiny object that showed my reflection, I'd stare sadly at the chubby girl looking back at me.

I started looking for "Get thin quick" diets. I planned the great wardrobes that I would buy when I lost weight. But I never seemed to make it past Day 3 of the 30-day plans. I never stuck to them because they could never accomplish what I wanted: to wake up one morning, thin and happy.

Toward the end of 8th grade, I decided to do something besides fantasize about how I wanted to look. A friend, who was also overweight, and I decided that we would go away for the summer and come back to 9th grade very thin. When school let out, I left for camp.

When I got there and saw the food, I didn't think that I would be able to keep up my end of the bargain. Even though there were four lunch lines serving different foods, everything was either fried and soaked in oil, or fried and soaked in oil with cheese on top. And at the end of every line, they had what was basically an ice cream store. There were so many different flavors and cones that it seemed almost sinful to let it go to waste.

After about a week, I signed up for a step aerobics class. It was either that, ballroom dancing with a bunch of pubescent, acne-covered boys, or sitting in the weight room all day, waiting for the macho guys to finish hogging the equipment. I started doing aerobics for an hour every day.

At the end of the day, I would add up all of the calories that I had burned by exercising. That made me feel so good that I decided to try skipping the ice cream at lunch. After I did, I felt so proud of myself that the next day I wanted to go even further. I decided to skip the ice cream at dinner, too.

It became like a dare for me. How far could I go before I cracked? Could I stand the pressure? I ate a little bit less each day. At the end of two weeks, I had lost 6 lbs. It wasn't that much but I already felt as if all my clothes were loose on me. I felt prettier and thinner.

After getting home from camp, I continued my dieting. Losing weight became like a game. I wanted to see how many pounds I could lose and how fast. When my body craved ice cream, I would try to ignore the sensation and force Jello down my throat instead. I tried to fill up my day with activities so that I wouldn't have time to think about food. At the end of the day, I would count up the calories I had consumed and feel proud that I had been able to resist temptation. It was this feeling that kept me going.

When I started high school that fall, I began playing volleyball. Since I was exercising vigorously, I continued to lose weight steadily. By the end of the season, I had lost 17 lbs and reached my ideal weight. At least that was my doctor's opinion. But I still wasn't satisfied.

I wanted to keep losing weight but, after volleyball season ended, the pounds no longer rolled off quite so effortlessly. I worried that I would become fat again. At the same time, I began to miss candy bars and ice cream pops. It had been almost five months since I had eaten a piece of chocolate and carrots had lost their appeal as a snack food. That's when I discovered the wonderful world of fat-free eating. Candy, cookies, and even some types of ice cream were available in fat-free varieties. For a while, I became a fat-free addict.

I saw every piece of food, no matter how low in calories, as something that would cause me to gain weight.

Unfortunately, fat-free food tastes like crap, so eventually I stopped eating it. I began to think of other ways to cut down my fat consumption, such as becoming a vegetarian and skipping meals. If I ate three full meals a day, I felt bad about myself.

In the spring, I joined the track team because I thought that I needed to lose more weight for shorts season. I would run between three and five miles a day. But the more weight I lost, the more unhappy I was with the way I looked. I was too thin in some places and too fat in others. I would spend hours in front of the mirror looking at each part of my body, finding flaws. Every time I passed a window or shiny object, I checked my reflection to see if my thighs had gotten any bigger since morning.

I started feeling guilty about everything I ate. My parents would take me out for pizza. After just one slice (that I had blotted all the oil off of) I would feel fat. I saw every piece of food, no matter how low in calories, as something that would cause me to gain weight. After eating, I would touch my stomach to see if it had gotten any bigger; I felt like the food was gathering up in little folds across my waist.

One night, I had to make peanut butter cookies for a school bake sale. I tasted part of one cookie in each batch to see if they were cooked or not. It was such a small amount of cookie, but afterwards I began to have that familiar feeling of fat growing in my body. It was 10 p.m., but I began doing crunches. I did more than 200 crunches that night. Doing the crunches themselves wasn't the bad part, it was the fact that I felt that eating even one cookie was a sin. I thought that I had broken a promise to myself to be thin.

The original idea of pushing myself to the limit was still present in my mind. I wanted to see how far I could go before I had to stop. I wanted to see what it would take for my willpower to crack, for my brain to cry, "Enough!"

One day I had an English muffin with nothing on it and a glass of water for breakfast, and fat-free cereal with skim milk and an apple for lunch. After school, I ran three miles on less than 300 calories. Considering all the calories I burned by running, I was in bad shape afterwards. I felt very dizzy. All the blood rushed to my head, and I thought that I was going to black out. But I still didn't feel like I had gone too far.

When I jokingly told a friend about the incident, he gave me a funny look and said, "That's not a good idea. Don't ever do it again." He wasn't the only one who thought I was overdoing it. A lot of my friends were getting tired of the fact that I wouldn't eat at McDonald's and that I made comments about the fat content in the food they ate. My parents had begun to complain that I was becoming too skinny and that my bones were sticking out. Then one day my best friend said to me, "You really are beginning to look anorexic."

Not long after that there was a week when I lost a pound a day. Suddenly, my parents' comments about my becoming unhealthy started echoing in my head. Losing 7 pounds in one week wasn't normal, it was frightening. It was the kind of thing that happened in TV movies about anorexia. I was afraid to get back on the scale because I didn't want to find out that I had lost another pound.

For the first time in a year, I looked in the mirror and really saw myself. My wrists had become scrawny and I was losing my hips. This wasn't the image that I had in mind when I started out. I had wanted to look slim and in shape, but instead I looked emaciated and bony. I had thought my friends were out of line when they said that I was worrying too much about what I ate. Now, I realized that they had been right.

Denying myself the food I wanted had become such a big part of my life that I couldn't imagine getting through the day without it. If I was going to get over that, I had to stop believing that every piece of food I put in my mouth would automatically make me fat. I had to recognize that since I was much more phys-ically active now than when I was young and chubby, I didn't have to starve myself to stay in shape. I had to realize that what I was becoming was not attractive. Being overly skinny was just as bad as being overweight. And the people around me had begun to get annoyed and even repulsed by the way I was so concerned about my appearance.

I will always be glad that I was able to lose weight, and I think that initially I had the right idea. I started by eating less junk food and exercising more, both of which are healthy things to do. But then I let myself get caught up in the fantasy of becoming some sort of supermodel. I became so obsessed with losing weight that I lost touch with reality. To get over that, I had to start listening to the people around me. I had to hear them when they told me that it was OK to eat a full meal. I had to start believing them when they said I wasn't fat.

I wish I could say that I was completely cured. I wish I could say that I have stopped checking nutrition labels and counting calories. But happily ever after doesn't come so easy. There are still days when guilt washes over me after I eat a full meal. I have to stop and remind myself that it's OK. But each day the guilt becomes smaller and easier to deal with.

And then there are the good days, when I don't think about my weight at all.

Renu was 16 when she wrote this story.

Marked at Birth

By Cynthia Orbes

Before I had my first operation three years ago, my face had a big birth defect. It looked wrinkly and sagged down like old dead skin. It was redder when I was younger. I was just born with it. I always wished that it wasn't there.

I first realized that this mark set me apart from other people when I was in kindergarten and kids would ask me about it.

They weren't just curious. People judged me for how it looked. Once I was on the bus and a girl said, "Ew, she better turn around, that ugly girl." I felt like I should not have been on the bus, like I should leave or just stay home.

Another time I was at the library and there was a group of guys sitting across from me. One of them said, "Look at that girl over there, she has a disease." They all started laughing. I was about to cry. I felt so unwelcome, like I should not be at the library either.

Part of me felt angry, wondering, "Why do I have to take this stress from these people who are ignorant and arrogant to think that they can make fun of me?" Another part of me felt sad. I would think to myself, "It's not my fault. I didn't intend for this to happen. I came out wrong—why me?"

I felt different from everyone else. Usually I wouldn't cry, because I thought of myself as strong. But I think that I did once or twice.

When I was younger my mom was trying to set up an operation to fix the mark on my face, but she never got to it because things got out of hand at home. We got kicked out of our apartment and had to move. Then I guess she forgot about it, or maybe she didn't think I cared about how I looked because I never mentioned how I felt.

I didn't want to bring it up because I knew my mother would feel bad about not being able to do anything, because she really didn't have a lot of money to spend on an operation. I also didn't want to tell my mother how I felt because she seemed like she was under a lot of pressure from everyone in the family, and I didn't think she'd want to hear my complaints on top of that.

If I notice any stares, I just try to think about things that make me happy, like books and music.

I've always tried to keep my emotions to myself. I just don't think that people should have to hear other people's problems if they can't help them, because it will just make them feel bad. I don't want other people to feel bad because I'm feeling bad.

So I didn't tell anyone how I felt about my mark. I didn't even write down how I felt, because I hoped that in the future I wouldn't look bad. I figured that one day I'd have an operation and after my operation I would feel very good, and I would not want to think about all of the times that I was feeling sad about my face. So I just tried to think of the good times I'd have after my operation, and how much better I would look.

I think my sister knew how I felt, though. Sometimes I would say, "I'm ugly," and she would say, "No, I am, look at my pointy nose." I would say that to her because hiding my feelings was difficult, and I couldn't take it anymore. I would tell her, "You're prettier than me," and she would say, "No, you're prettier than me." Then I would say, "Stop lying."

My friends and their mothers would say things to make me feel better, too. They would say things like, "You're very pretty and you're going to be even prettier when you grow up." It made me feel better in the moment, but sometimes I would still think, "They're just saying that." But they weren't.

When I was 10, my mother died and my sister and I went into foster care. Around that time I met a woman who became a great friend and a mentor. She always told me that the mark didn't look that bad, but she convinced me that I should get an operation. She said, "It won't be that bad. I'll take you there and your sister and I will be with you the whole time. When you wake up I'll buy you ice cream and whatever you want."

I did want the operation, because I wanted to look better. So she set it up and the foster care agency paid for it. But I was so scared before the operation. I thought they were going to mess me up or even kill me by mistake. I did not trust the doctors. I was 10 and I thought crazy things.

When the day came I was so scared. I didn't want to believe it was happening and I just wanted to get it over with. I thought to myself, "No whining or complaining. I am doing this and that's it."

While getting put to sleep I was thinking, "Will I die? Will I ever wake up and move my body and look at nature and beauty again? Is once always enough for everything?" I was terrified, but I guess I seemed brave because the doctors told me I was.

The doctors sliced my lip going down to the left of my face

and cut a little and stretched my lip so it could look smoother. They also cut in the center of my lip and lifted the skin higher so my lip would not sag.

After the operation my lip was so swollen it looked twice as bad as before. After a couple of months, though, the skin healed. Now it looks thinner and a little smoother than before. I knew my face would not look perfect, but I'm relieved that the mark is not as noticeable.

Now I don't feel that my mark is the first thing that people see. Usually, people don't stare at me anymore. If I notice any stares, I just try to think about things that make me happy, like books and music and all my friends who care about me.

I wish that when I was younger, and my mark was worse, I could have cared less what people thought and said about me. But I was not able to stop caring what people thought about me until after I got the operation. Knowing that I looked better made me feel more confident, and that helped me ignore what people thought of me. Even so, it took me about two years after the first operation to stop feeling so self-conscious.

As my face began to heal, I realized how many negative feelings that mark had given me about myself, and how much more positive I've been feeling. It took a long time, but I stopped thinking about how bad I looked and instead focused on how much better I look.

Knowing that I looked better made me feel more confident, and that helped me ignore what people thought of me.

If I hadn't had this done I would not even try to look pretty, because I would think, "Forget it, who wants to know me." Now, I look in the mirror and I think it's amazing that I feel so much prettier.

Feeling better about my face gave me more confidence to act how I want to act and express who I am. When I was younger my face sometimes held me back from acting silly. I was not timid, exactly, but I was ticked off that people stared at me and I tried not to attract attention. I wanted to be like everyone else—normal.

Often I still feel angry that people judged me and made those comments. I try really hard not to act like that toward anyone. I know how much it hurts.

These days, I am much more able to ignore what people say. And I'm letting myself loose more. I've also started to wear clothes that people notice—wearing all black, and dying my hair. It feels better to attract attention this way. Instead of noticing my birth mark, I want people to think, "That girl looks cool."

Cynthia was 15 when she wrote this story. She graduated from high school and attended college in New York City.

Jamaal Pascall

Life As a Shorty

By SaeRom Park

Last year, I was walking up a ramp in the subway station when a concerned young man approached me. "Little girl, are you lost?" he asked. I felt like telling him to bug off, but instead, I gave him a polite smile and said, "No, are you?"

I was 14 years old at the time. I'm 15 now, but it doesn't matter. Random people still approach me thinking I'm a little girl. It's true I do look young, and being only 5' tall doesn't help.

Three years ago, in 7th grade, when I first entered the doors of my new school, most of the kids were shorter than 5'2". Boy, did I fit right in. Those were the good old days. The tall people were the oddballs and I was normal.

Even some of the guys were shorter than I was and that meant that I could push them around. And I was only 4'10"! Sonny, a good friend of mine, was a good two inches shorter than me. I remember I used to say to him sweetly, "Sonny could you get me a glass of water?" and he'd look up at me and say, "Sure." The power of being taller than a guy was exhilarating.

But guess what? At 5'9", Sonny is now towering over me and will no longer succumb to my whims. Recently, when I asked him to get a book from a high shelf that I couldn't reach, he replied teasingly, "Go get it yourself, Shorty."

I felt helpless and...short. While he had grown at the rate of about four inches a year, I have grown maybe two inches total. In three years! Even my girlfriends have deserted me, shooting to 5'3"and up. By the end of 7th grade, everyone called me some variation of "shorty" and I was forever branded.

Every morning I wake up and realize that it's another frustrating day battling an anti-short world. When I took the subway recently to meet my friend, I thought to myself, "Why don't they make the subway bars lower? Or at least put poles everywhere so I can hang onto something?"

I won't even get into how I toppled over an annoyed tall lady who, had she been standing, could have easily grabbed onto the bars that I couldn't quite reach. Then, when I finally got out of the train, I got totally trampled by the herd of commuters who didn't even see me.

I had hoped to relax, hang out, and go clothes shopping with my friend, but I should have realized that that last part would infuriate me. OK, there are stores for large women and most other stores have things in large sizes. But, hello! What about the short people? Why is it that I have to scavenge for that last size 1 or 3 or else search for all the XXLs in the kids' section? My friends all passed this stage quickly, but I have yet to move on.

I'm afraid I will be eternally stuck in this dilemma. Can you imagine me in 30 years—a 45-year-old Korean lady rummaging through the racks of small and medium baby tees for her own clothes?

What's even worse is when being short makes me feel like a

kid and when I feel like I can't do certain things because of my height. I feel caged in by my shortness and begin to wish that I were tall.

Probably the worst thing for me about being short is that it's a huge disadvantage in athletics, especially in volleyball. My friends and I discovered the sport in 8th grade. We were all determined to become incredible athletes and join the high school volleyball team. It was exciting for me to be part of a team sport and I loved volleyball from the start. Since we were all beginners, my height didn't matter—at first.

A year and a half has passed since then and we're all still playing like we want to become pros. Despite my efforts, however, there is a noticeable difference between my friends and me on the court.

I cannot block, nor am I consistently able to "spike" the ball onto the opponents' court because, hey, I'm just too short. It doesn't matter that I can jump as high as some of the taller players; their height just adds so much more.

I have to scavenge for that last size 1 or 3 or search in the kids' section.

It helps that volleyball has a lot of other components, like passing and setting, so I work on what I can. And despite my shortness, I managed to play on the team last year.

Still, if I were taller, I'd devote my life to volleyball just for the chance of being able to play as a professional. But because I'm short, I know I'll never turn pro.

I guess I have accepted that being short is just a way of life. And I've learned to deal with it. I know the world won't become short-friendly overnight and my mission is definitely an upward battle (like everything else), but I'm beginning to adapt.

Last year, my friend Sonny would make fun of me. "So, how's the weather down there?" he'd ask. I never answered him back because I was too frustrated.

But now I feel like I can just look up at him and say, "It's fine, just fine. It gets a little rainy down here sometimes but it's OK 'cause the sun's shining now."

SaeRom was 15 when she wrote this story. She later graduated from Williams College and became a political organizer.

Frank Malkum

Learning to Love My Hair

By Charlene George

A few weeks after I was put in foster care, my foster mother told me I was going to get my hair cut. I was 7 years old, and I couldn't remember ever getting my hair cut before. I had no image of what it would look like.

We went into a Spanish hair salon, and I saw lots of happy people coming out. I was sitting there saying to myself, "I hope I am going to be one of those happy people." But when I saw people's hair falling to the floor, my chin dropped. I was scared.

"Come on baby, you're next," they said. They turned me to where I could not see the mirror. I could hear the scissors slapping toward my hair and I saw so much hair falling down. I was worried, asking, "Why do you have to cut so much hair?"

My foster mother told me to sit and be quiet. The man said, "Trust me, it's going to look nice."

When he finished, he turned my chair around and I looked in the mirror. I wanted to cry, but I didn't want my foster mother to yell at me. It was too short—it only came halfway down my forehead. I was not very pleased, knowing it was too late now to take back my OK.

The other people waiting to get their hair done told me it looked nice. But I wasn't sure. I felt like a different person. The main thing on my mind was how all the people at school would react.

The next morning, I couldn't wait to get to school to see what everyone would think. I did my best with my hair and got on the bus. But then I started to feel nervous. I worried that the kids at my school were not going to like it.

A lot of people noticed my haircut, and one teacher told me how nice my hair looked. Then it happened. There was this group who thought they were so cool. They always had something bad to say about others to put them down. They'd say things like, "Look at that fat girl," or they'd make fun of someone for not having on some name brand clothes or sneakers.

As soon as they saw my new haircut they started laughing and saying mean things. I was so hurt. They really had a lot of jokes for me, laughing and pointing their fingers.

If I had a card for every day I was laughed at, I'd have a full deck.

I thought it was going to stop there, but it didn't. I hated having people judge me by my hair. They pointed at my head and called me bald, and even made a song about it at lunch.

The song went something like: "You're a bald-headed chick-chick, you ain't got no hair in the back, gel up, weave up, your hair is messed up." It bothered me so much I would leave the lunchroom or my classroom and cry my heart out in the school bathroom.

Eventually, my hair started to grow out, but that didn't stop people from making fun of me. And whenever my foster mother decided I needed another haircut, I got one. I didn't have a choice.

I used to hate to feel myself break down when people were

being negative about my hairstyle. It made me feel so down on myself that I started to believe I was ugly, that no one cared and that the world was against me. I felt like a piece of bread that a whole lot of birds were trying to feed off of.

I knew that the kids at school were not going to stop joking on me, so I had to plan something for myself to stop feeling the way I did.

For a while, I would try to fight back. I would make fun of how the other kids looked, too, like how one of the guys had birthmarks all over his head that looked like ringworm. I also did things like throw spitballs, curse people out, or just fight.

Doing things like that made me feel better, but then I would get sent to the time-out room or get suspended for a few days. I was going to start failing my classes if I didn't change my act.

One day I asked myself if I was really ugly like they said. My answer was no. I hadn't been ugly when my hair was long, so why should I be ugly now?

I decided that I was not going to let the other kids provoke me into getting in trouble. I was going to choose the words that came out of my mouth wisely. I had to grow up and stop letting the things people said about me get to me.

Of course, that was easier said than done. It took me years to build up my confidence. But by the time I was around 16, I was ready to make some changes with my hair. I knew I was getting more mature, so I wanted to try new looks. And I just wanted to feel cool for once.

I started dying my hair and tried all different colors: black, light brown and dark brown, hazelnut, and orange mixed with red. I also put things in my hair like braids, and even some human hair. I even wore my hair short with wet-and-go curls at one point.

Sometimes other people liked my hair, and sometimes they didn't. But I was happy trying all those new hairstyles. And wearing my hair in ways that fit my body improved my self-esteem, even though I was still being bothered by other kids in school.

If I had a card for every day I was laughed at, I'd have a full deck, but I decided I was just going to have to let them play out.

Sometimes I would still cry or I would tell them things like, "I'm still going to have a wonderful day," holding a smile when I said it. Telling myself I looked good and not ugly kept me feeling positive about myself, even when people made remarks.

Another thing that helped me were two supportive teachers: Ms. Epps and Ms. Elliot. I looked up to them and thought of them as my stepmothers. They loved my hairstyles. They'd tell me my styles went with my features and made me look like an African princess. Listening to all the positive things they had to say made me feel better.

Responding to mean comments by saying good things, or nothing at all, makes me feel happy.

Now I'm 18, and when people bother me I try not to listen to them. I can feel that what's important is not what anyone else likes about me but what I like about myself. I've put in a lot of effort to feel comfortable with how I look.

Now I hold my head high and make sure my hair is looking fine. When people make comments I'll say something like, "God blessed me just like he will do for you, and have a blessed day."

They may look at me like I'm crazy and say they do not believe in God, but I just walk away and do not pay them any mind. Responding to mean comments by saying good things, or nothing at all, makes me feel happy.

These days I still change up my hairstyle a lot. I like making my own choices about how I look.

I sometimes go to the extreme, like when I cut all my hair off last summer, even shorter than what my foster mother did when I was 7 years old. I didn't really want to go bald, but my hair was falling out because of the chemicals and hair dyes I put in it.

But I worked my bald hair cut with confidence. I accessorized with a head scarf, and when people asked me why I cut my hair,

I would just explain it to them and they understood.

I spent a long time beating myself up and not liking my hair just because someone else did not like it. It makes me feel good now to let everyone know that I am going to wear my hair however I want. Other people may like it or not, but I won't change it for anyone but me.

Charlene was 19 when she wrote this story.

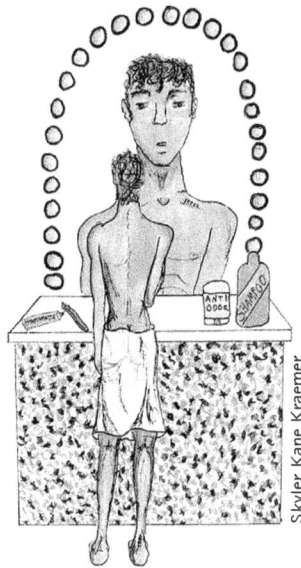

Skyler Kane Kraemer

Finding Your Confidence

We all know that looking your best makes you feel good. But when it comes to confidence, how much does appearance really matter? We talked to Dr. Lori Evans, a clinical psychologist at the New York University Child Study Center, to find out.

—Reporting by Angel Muñoz

Q: What is confidence?

A: You can have confidence about one thing, like feeling confident that you're a good soccer player, or that you have a pretty face, but you may not feel good about yourself in general.

In psychology, we look at confidence as a general idea about self—that you feel good about who you are as a person, that you're able to rely on yourself and you have faith in your own ability to make good judgments and good decisions for yourself.

Q: How can your appearance affect your confidence?

A: I think your appearance can have a huge impact on how you feel and your sense of who you are. But it's not so much your objective appearance—it's more how you feel about the way you look.

For instance, someone who's not that attractive, but who enjoys who they are and how they look, can have a lot more confidence than a really attractive person who doesn't feel good about themselves. And you can see that in the way they carry themselves.

If people have a really good self-image, than they don't need things like the most expensive clothes. They can create their own style.

Q: Do teens worry about their appearance more than kids or adults do?

A: Unfortunately, yes. When you're little, other people are dressing you, and you don't have control over it. And when you're an adult, your sense of style is more settled. But I think adolescence is a time when kids are defining themselves, and sometimes they do that from the outside in, using a certain look to show that they're part of a certain group. Teens in particular use style and fashion to define themselves.

Emphasize the things you like about yourself.

Also, when you're a teen, your body goes through drastic changes. It's the time when you start getting acne, when girls are developing (or not developing) breasts—all kinds of changes that can make you feel uncomfortable, and that other people notice and might comment on, which can make you even more uncomfortable.

Q: What can you do to feel better about the way you look?

A: There are some things we can change about our looks and some things we can't. Find little things that make you feel good—a favorite shirt, or a nice hair clip if you like the way your hair looks. Sometimes you can use those kinds of things to emphasize the things you like about yourself and put your personality out there.

You definitely want to make efforts to feel good about how you look. Eating well and exercising can help—crash diets won't. When you take care of your body, you feel better about yourself.

And the more you value yourself, the more that kind of confidence comes with it. It does take hard work. Teens should look in the mirror and make positive statements about things they like about themselves. Sometimes kids do get very negative. In that case, having a friend or another person in their life who points out the positive things about them can be great.

Q: How can you maintain a positive self-image if other kids are teasing you?

A: Using humor, or assertiveness, (without escalating the situation) can be a great way to fend off teasing. If you're not comfortable enough to do that, try to surround yourself with people who can defend you and be there for you. And remind yourself about your positive qualities.

Q: What are some other ways a teen can increase his or her confidence?

A: Find something that you really love to do. You don't have to be the best—it's OK to try out for a part in a play even though you don't intend on being a Broadway actor, and maybe get a small part. Sometimes, just the flexibility of trying new things can help you feel better. Finding other things to feel good about can help you expand your sense of self beyond your appearance.

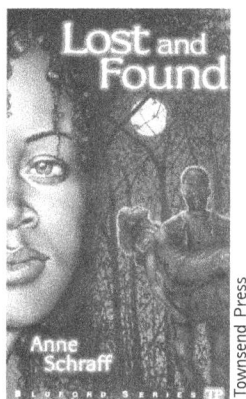

Townsend Press

Lost and Found

Darcy Wills winced at the loud rap music coming from her sister's room.

> My rhymes were rockin'
> MC's were droppin'
> People shoutin' and hip-hoppin'
> Step to me and you'll be inferior
> 'Cause I'm your lyrical superior.

Darcy went to Grandma's room. The darkened room smelled of lilac perfume, Grandma's favorite, but since her stroke Grandma did not notice it, or much of anything.

"Bye, Grandma," Darcy whispered from the doorway. "I'm going to school now."

Just then, the music from Jamee's room cut off, and Jamee rushed into the hallway.

The teen characters in the Bluford novels, a fiction series by Townsend Press, struggle with many of the same difficult issues as the writers in this book. Here's the first chapter from *Lost and Found*, by Anne Schraff, the first book in the series. In this novel, high school sophomore Darcy contends with the return of her long-absent father, the troubling behavior of her younger sister Jamee, and the beginning of her first relationship.

"Like she even hears you," Jamee said as she passed Darcy. Just two years younger than Darcy, Jamee was in eighth grade, though she looked older.

"It's still nice to talk to her. Sometimes she understands. You want to pretend she's not here or something?"

"She's not," Jamee said, grabbing her backpack.

"Did you study for your math test?" Darcy asked. Mom was an emergency room nurse who worked rotating shifts. Most of the time, Mom was too tired to pay much attention to the girls' schoolwork. So Darcy tried to keep track of Jamee.

"Mind your own business," Jamee snapped.

"You got two D's on your last report card," Darcy scolded. "You wanna flunk?" Darcy did not want to sound like a nagging parent, but Jamee wasn't doing her best. Maybe she couldn't make A's like Darcy, but she could do better.

Jamee stomped out of the apartment, slamming the door behind her. "Mom's trying to get some rest!" Darcy yelled. "Do you have to be so selfish?" But Jamee was already gone, and the apartment was suddenly quiet.

Darcy loved her sister. Once, they had been good friends. But now all Jamee cared about was her new group of rowdy friends. They leaned on cars outside of school and turned up rap music on their boom boxes until the street seemed to tremble like an earthquake. Jamee had even stopped hanging out with her old friend Alisha Wrobel, something she used to do every weekend.

Darcy went back into the living room, where her mother sat in the recliner sipping coffee. "I'll be home at 2:30, Mom," Darcy said. Mom smiled faintly. She was tired, always tired. And lately she was worried too. The hospital where she worked was cutting staff. It seemed each day fewer people were expected to do more work. It was like trying to climb a mountain that keeps getting taller as you go. Mom was forty-four, but just yesterday she said, "I'm like an old car that's run out of warranty, baby. You know what happens then. Old car is ready for the junk heap. Well, maybe that hospital is gonna tell me one of these days—'Mattie Mae Wills, we don't need you anymore. We can get somebody younger and cheaper.'"

"Mom, you're not old at all," Darcy had said, but they were only words, empty words. They could not erase the dark, weary lines from beneath her mother's eyes.

Darcy headed down the street toward Bluford High School. It was not a terrible neighborhood they lived in; it just was not good. Many front yards were not cared for. Debris—fast food wrappers, plastic bags, old newspapers—blew around and piled against fences and curbs. Darcy hated that. Sometimes she and other kids from school spent Saturday mornings cleaning up, but it seemed a losing battle. Now, as she walked, she tried to focus on small spots of beauty along the way. Mrs. Walker's pink and white roses bobbed proudly in the morning breeze. The Hustons' rock garden was carefully designed around a wooden windmill.

As she neared Bluford, Darcy thought about the science project that her biology teacher, Ms. Reed, was assigning. Darcy was doing hers on tidal pools. She was looking forward to visiting a real tidal pool, taking pictures, and doing research. Today, Ms. Reed would be dividing the students into teams of two. Darcy wanted to be paired with her close friend, Brisana Meeks. They were both excellent students, a cut above most kids at Bluford, Darcy thought.

"Today, we are forming project teams so that each student can gain something valuable from the other," Ms. Reed said as Darcy sat at her desk. Ms. Reed was a tall, stately woman who reminded Darcy of the Statue of Liberty. She would have been a perfect model for the statue if Lady Liberty had been a black woman. She never would have been called pretty, but it was possible she might have been called a handsome woman. "For this assignment, each of you will be working with someone you've never worked with before."

Darcy was worried. If she was not teamed with Brisana,

maybe she would be teamed with some really dumb student who would pull her down. Darcy was a little ashamed of herself for thinking that way. Grandma used to say that all flowers are equal, but different. The simple daisy was just as lovely as the prize rose. But still Darcy did not want to be paired with some weak partner who would lower her grade.

"Darcy Wills will be teamed with Tarah Carson," Ms. Reed announced.

Darcy gasped. Not Tarah! Not that big, chunky girl with the brassy voice who squeezed herself into tight skirts and wore lime green or hot pink satin tops and cheap jewelry. Not Tarah who hung out with Cooper Hodden, that loser who was barely hanging on to his football eligibility. Darcy had heard that Cooper had been left back once or twice and even got his driver's license as a sophomore. Darcy's face felt hot with anger. Why was Ms. Reed doing this?

Hakeem Randall, a handsome, shy boy who sat in the back row, was teamed with the class blabbermouth, LaShawn Appleby. Darcy had a secret crush on Hakeem since freshman year. So far she had only shared this with her diary, never with another living soul.

It was almost as though Ms. Reed was playing some devilish game. Darcy glanced at Tarah, who was smiling broadly. Tarah had an enormous smile, and her teeth contrasted harshly with her dark red lipstick. "Great," Darcy muttered under her breath.

Ms. Reed ord e red the teams to meet so they could begin to plan their projects.

As she sat down by Tarah, Darcy was instantly sickened by a syrupy-sweet odor.

She must have doused herself with cheap perfume this morning , Darcy thought.

"Hey, girl," Tarah said. "Well, don't you look down in the mouth. What's got you lookin' that way?"

It was hard for Darcy to meet new people, especially someone like Tarah, a person Aunt Charlotte would call "low class." These were people who were loud and rude. They drank too much, used drugs, got into fights and ruined the neighborhood. They yelled ugly insults at people, even at their friends. Darcy did not actually know that Tarah did anything like this personally, but she seemed like the type who did.

"I just didn't think you'd be interested in tidal pools," Darcy explained.

Tarah slammed her big hand on the desk, making her gold bracelets jangle like ice cubes in a glass, and laughed. Darcy had never heard a mule bray, but she was sure it made exactly the same sound. Then Tarah leaned close and whispered, "Girl, I don't know a tidal pool from a fool. Ms. Reed stuck us together to mess with our heads, you hear what I'm sayin'?"

"Maybe we could switch to other partners," Darcy said nervously.

A big smile spread slowly over Tarah's face. "Nah, I think I'm gonna enjoy this. You're always sittin' here like a princess collecting your A's. Now you gotta work with a regular person, so you better loosen up, girl!"

Darcy felt as if her teeth were glued to her tongue. She fumbled in her bag for her outline of the project. It all seemed like a horrible joke now. She and Tarah Carson standing knee-deep in the muck of a tidal pool!

"Worms live there, don't they?" Tarah asked, twisting a big gold ring on her chubby finger.

"Yeah, I guess," Darcy replied.

"Big green worms," Tarah continued. "So if you get your feet stuck in the bottom of that old tidal pool, and you can't get out, do the worms crawl up your clothes?"

Darcy ignored the remark. "I'd like for us to go there soon, you know, look around."

"My boyfriend, Cooper, he goes down to the ocean all the time. He can take us. He says he's seen these fiddler crabs. They look like big spiders, and they'll try to bite your toes off. Cooper says so," Tarah said.

"Stop being silly," Darcy shot back. "If you're not even going to be serious . . . "

"You think you're better than me, don't you?" Tarah suddenly growled.

"I never said—" Darcy blurted.

"You don't have to say it, girl. It's in your eyes. You think I'm a low-life and you're something special. Well, I got more friends than you got fingers and toes together. You got no friends, and everybody laughs at you behind your back. Know what the word on you is? Darcy Wills give you the chills."

Just then, the bell rang, and Darcy was glad for the excuse to turn away from Tarah, to hide the hot tears welling in her eyes. She quickly rushed from the classroom, relieved that school was over. Darcy did not think she could bear to sit through another class just now.

Darcy headed down the long street towards home. She did not like Tarah. Maybe it was wrong, but it was true. Still, Tarah's brutal words hurt. Even stupid, awful people might tell you the truth about yourself. And Darcy did not have any real friends, except for Brisana. Maybe the other kids were mocking her behind her back. Darcy was very slender, not as shapely as many of the other girls. She remembered the time when Cooper Hodden was hanging in front of the deli with his friends, and he yelled as Darcy went by, "Hey, is that really a female there? Sure don't look like it. Looks more like an old broomstick with hair. " His companions laughed rudely, and Darcy had walked a little faster.

A terrible thought clawed at Darcy. Maybe she was the loser, not Tarah. Tarah was always hanging with a bunch of kids, laughing and joking. She would go down the hall to the lockers and greetings would come from everywhere. "Hey, Tarah!" "What's up, Tar?" "See ya at lunch, girl." When Darcy went to the lockers, there was dead silence.

Darcy usually glanced into stores on her way home from school. She enjoyed looking at the trays of chicken feet and pork ears at the little Asian grocery store. Sometimes she would even steal a glance at the diners sitting by the picture window at the Golden Grill Restaurant. But today she stared straight ahead, her shoulders drooping.

If this had happened last year, she would have gone directly to Grandma's house, a block from where Darcy lived. How many times had Darcy and Jamee run to Grandma's, eaten applesauce cookies, drunk cider, and poured out their troubles to Grandma. Somehow, their problems would always dissolve in the warmth of her love and wisdom. But now Grandma was a frail figure in the corner of their apartment, saying little. And what little she did say made less and less sense.

Darcy was usually the first one home. The minute she got there, Mom left for the hospital to take the 3:00 to 11:00 shift in the ER. By the time Mom finished her paperwork at the hospital, she would be lucky to be home again by midnight. After Mom left, Darcy went to Grandma's room to give her the malted nutrition drink that the doctor ordered her to have three times a day.

"Want to drink your chocolate malt, Grandma?" Darcy asked, pulling up a chair beside Grandma's bed.

Grandma was sitting up, and her eyes were open. "No. I'm not hungry," she said listlessly. She always said that.

"You need to drink your malt, Grandma," Darcy insisted, gently putting the straw between the pinched lips.

Grandma sucked the malt slowly. "Grandma, nobody likes me at school," Darcy said. She did not expect any response. But there was a strange comfort in telling Grandma anyway. "Everybody laughs at me. It's because I'm shy and maybe stuck-up, too, I guess. But I don't mean to be. Stuck-up, I mean. Maybe I'm weird. I could be weird, I guess. I could be like Aunt Charlotte . . ." Tears rolled down Darcy's cheeks. Her heart ached with loneliness. There was nobody to talk to anymore, nobody who had time to listen, nobody who understood.

Grandma blinked and pushed the straw away. Her eyes brightened as they did now and then. "You are a wonderful girl. Everybody knows that," Grandma said in an almost normal voice. It happened like that sometimes. It was like being in the middle of a dark storm and having the clouds part, revealing a patch of clear, sunlit blue. For just a few precious minutes, Grandma was bright-eyed and saying normal things.

"Oh, Grandma, I'm so lonely," Darcy cried, pressing her head against Grandma's small shoulder.

"You were such a beautiful baby," Grandma said, stroking her hair." 'That one is going to shine like the morning star.' That's what I told your Mama. 'That child is going to shine like the morning star.' Tell me, Angelcake, is your daddy home yet?"

Darcy straightened. "Not yet." Her heart pounded so hard, she could feel it thumping in her chest. Darcy's father had not been home in five years.

"Well, tell him to see me when he gets home. I want him to buy you that blue dress you liked in the store window. That's for you, Angelcake. Tell him I've got money. My social security came, you know. I have money for the blue dress," Grandma said, her eyes slipping shut.

Just then, Darcy heard the apartment door slam. Jamee had come home. Now she stood in the hall, her hands belligerently on her hips. "Are you talking to Grandma again?" Jamee demanded.

"She was talking like normal," Darcy said. "Sometimes she does. You know she does."

"That is so stupid," Jamee snapped. "She never says anything right anymore. Not anything!" Jamee's voice trembled.

Darcy got up quickly and set down the can of malted milk. She ran to Jamee and put her arms around her sister. "Jamee, I know you're hurting too."

"Oh, don't be stupid," Jamee protested, but Darcy hugged her more tightly, and in a few seconds Jamee was crying. "She was the best thing in this stupid house," Jamee cried. "Why'd she have to go?"

"She didn't go," Darcy said. "Not really."

"She did! She did!" Jamee sobbed. She struggled free of Darcy, ran to her room, and slammed the door. In a minute, Darcy heard the bone-rattling sound of rap music.

Teens:
How to Get More Out of This Book

Self-help: The teens who wrote the stories in this book did so because they hope that telling their stories will help readers who are facing similar challenges. They want you to know that you are not alone, and that taking specific steps can help you manage or overcome very difficult situations. They've done their best to be clear about the actions that worked for them so you can see if they'll work for you.

Writing: You can also use the book to improve your writing skills. Each teen in this book wrote 5-10 drafts of his or her story before it was published. If you read the stories closely you'll see that the teens work to include a beginning, a middle, and an end, and good scenes, description, dialogue, and anecdotes (little stories). To improve your writing, take a look at how these writers construct their stories. Try some of their techniques in your own writing.

Reading: Finally, you'll notice that we include the first chapter from a Bluford Series novel in this book, alongside the true stories by teens. We hope you'll like it enough to continue reading. The more you read, the more you'll strengthen your reading skills. Teens at Youth Communication like the Bluford novels because they explore themes similar to those in their own stories. Your school may already have the Bluford books. If not, you can order them online for only $1.

Resources on the Web

We will occasionally post Think About It questions on our website, www.youthcomm.org, to accompany stories in this and other Youth Communication books. We try out the questions with teens and post the ones they like best. Many teens report that writing answers to those questions in a journal is very helpful.

How to Use This Book in Staff Training

Staff say that reading these stories gives them greater insight into what teens are thinking and feeling, and new strategies for working with them. You can help the staff you work with by using these stories as case studies.

Select one story to read in the group, and ask staff to identify and discuss the main issue facing the teen. There may be disagreement about this, based on the background and experience of staff. That is fine. One point of the exercise is that teens have complex lives and needs. Adults can probably be more effective if they don't focus too narrowly and can see several dimensions of their clients.

Ask staff: What issues or feelings does the story provoke in them? What kind of help do they think the teen wants? What interventions are likely to be most promising? Least effective? Why? How would you build trust with the teen writer? How have other adults failed the teen, and how might that affect his or her willingness to accept help? What other resources would be helpful to this teen, such as peer support, a mentor, counseling, family therapy, etc.

Resources on the Web

From time to time we will post Think About It questions on our website, www.youthcomm.org, to accompany stories in this and other Youth Communication books. We try out the questions with teens and post the ones that they find most effective. We'll also post lesson for some of the stories. Adults can use the questions and lessons in workshops.

Teachers and Staff:
How to Use This Book in Groups

When working with teens individually or in groups, you can use these stories can help young people face difficult issues in a way that feels safe to them. That's because talking about the issues in the stories usually feels safer to teens than talking about those same issues in their own lives. Addressing issues through the stories allows for some personal distance; they hit close to home, but not too close. Talking about them opens up a safe place for reflection. As teens gain confidence talking about the issues in the stories, they usually become more comfortable talking about those issues in their own lives.

Below are general questions to guide your discussion. In most cases you can read a story and conduct a discussion in one 45-minute session. Teens are usually happy to read the stories aloud, with each teen reading a paragraph or two. (Allow teens to pass if they don't want to read.) It takes 10-15 minutes to read a story straight through. However, it is often more effective to let workshop participants make comments and discuss the story as you go along. The workshop leader may even want to annotate her copy of the story beforehand with key questions.

If teens read the story ahead of time or silently, it's good to break the ice with a few questions that get everyone on the same page: Who is the main character? How old is she? What happened to her? How did she respond? Another good starting question is: "What stood out for you in the story?" Go around the room and let each person briefly mention one thing.

Then move on to open-ended questions, which encourage participants to think more deeply about what the writers were feeling, the choices they faced, and they actions they took. There are no right or wrong answers to the open-ended questions.

Open-ended questions encourage participants to think about how the themes, emotions, and choices in the stories relate to their own lives. Here are some examples of open-ended questions that we have found to be effective. You can use variations of these questions with almost any story in this book.

—What main problem or challenge did the writer face?

—What choices did the teen have in trying to deal with the problem?

—Which way of dealing with the problem was most effective for the teen? Why?

—What strengths, skills, or resources did the teen use to address the challenge?

—If you were in the writer's shoes, what would you have done?

—What could adults have done better to help this young person?

—What have you learned by reading this story that you didn't know before?

—What, if anything, will you do differently after reading this story?

—What surprised you in this story?

—Do you have a different view of this issue, or see a different way of dealing with it, after reading this story? Why or why not?

Credits

The stories in this book originally appeared in the following
Youth Communication publications:

"The Puberty Plague," by Marlene Peralta, *New Youth Connections*, April 1998; "Big Breasts Are No Blessing," by Rasheeda Raji, *New Youth Connections*, March 2001; "My Cups Are Half-Empty," by Andrea Guscott, *New Youth Connections*, November 2006; "Big, Black and Beautiful," by Anonymous, *New Youth Connections*, December 1997; "Lightening My Skin, Straightening My Hair," by Samantha Brown, *New Youth Connections*, September/October 1997; "When Nappy Didn't Make Me Happy," by Keshia Harrell, *New Youth Connections*, January/February 2003; "Who's That Girl?" by Danny Gong, *New Youth Connections*, September/October 1998; "Cover Girl," by Bashiyrah Morrow, *Represent*, November/December 2000; "I Was a Beauty School Sucker," by Tonya Leslie, *New Youth Connections*, June 1990; "Beauty or Beast?" By Lisa Markland, *New Youth Connections*, May 1993; "Trying Femininity on for Size," by Debbie Seraphin, *New Youth Connections*, March 1999; "Covering My Butt," by LaToya Souvenir, *New Youth Connections*, November 1995; "Naturally Thin," by Desiree Guery, *New Youth Connections*, September/October 2002; "Mirror, Mirror on the Wall," by I. Okolo, *Represent*, November/December 2000; "Beauty Is More Than Skin Deep," by Danielle Wilson, *Represent*, March/April 1998; "I Took Dieting Too Far," by Renu George, *New Youth Connections*, November 1996; "Marked at Birth," by Cynthia Orbes, *Represent*, September/October 2003; "Life As A Shortie," by SaeRom Park, *New Youth Connections*, September/October 1997; "Learning to Love My Hair," By Charlene George, *Represent*, May/June 2008; "Finding Your Confidence," *Represent*, May/June 2008.

About
Youth Communication

Youth Communication, founded in 1980, is a nonprofit youth development program located in New York City whose mission is to teach writing, journalism, and leadership skills. The teenagers we train become writers for our websites and books and for two print magazines: *New Youth Connections*, a general-interest youth magazine, and *Represent*, a magazine by and for young people in foster care.

Each year, up to 100 young people participate in Youth Communication's school-year and summer journalism workshops, where they work under the direction of full-time professional editors. Most are African-American, Latino, or Asian, and many are recent immigrants. The opportunity to reach their peers with accurate portrayals of their lives and important self-help information motivates the young writers to create powerful stories.

Our goal is to run a strong youth development program in which teens produce high quality stories that inform and inspire their peers. Doing so requires us to be sensitive to the complicated lives and emotions of the teen participants while also providing an intellectually rigorous experience. We achieve that goal in the writing/teaching/editing relationship, which is the core of our program.

Our teaching and editorial process begins with discussions

between adult editors and the teen staff. In those meetings, the teens and the editors work together to identify the most important issues in the teens' lives and to figure out how those issues can be turned into stories that will resonate with teen readers.

Once story topics are chosen, students begin the process of crafting their stories. For a personal story, that means revisiting events in one's past to understand their significance for the future. For a commentary, it means developing a logical and persuasive point of view. For a reported story, it means gathering information through research and interviews. Students look inward and outward as they try to make sense of their experiences and the world around them and find the points of intersection between personal and social concerns. That process can take a few weeks or a few months. Stories frequently go through ten or more drafts as students work under the guidance of their editors, the way any professional writer does.

Many of the students who walk through our doors have uneven skills, as a result of poor education, living under extremely stressful conditions, or coming from homes where English is a second language. Yet, to complete their stories, students must successfully perform a wide range of activities, including writing and rewriting, reading, discussion, reflection, research, interviewing, and typing. They must work as members of a team and they must accept individual responsibility. They learn to provide constructive criticism, and to accept it. They engage in explorations of truthfulness, fairness, and accuracy. They meet deadlines. They must develop the audacity to believe that they have something important to say and the humility to recognize that saying it well is not a process of instant gratification. Rather, it usually requires a long, hard struggle through many discussions and much rewriting.

It would be impossible to teach these skills and dispositions as separate, disconnected topics, like grammar, ethics, or assertiveness. However, we find that students make rapid progress when they are learning skills in the context of an inquiry that is personally significant to them and that will benefit their peers.

When teens publish their stories—in *New Youth Connections* and *Represent*, on the web, and in other publications—they reach tens of thousands of teen and adult readers. Teachers, counselors, social workers, and other adults circulate the stories to young people in their classes and out-of-school youth programs. Adults tell us that teens in their programs—including many who are ordinarily resistant to reading—clamor for the stories. Teen readers report that the stories give them information they can't get anywhere else, and inspire them to reflect on their lives and open lines of communication with adults.

Writers usually participate in our program for one semester, though some stay much longer. Years later, many of them report that working here was a turning point in their lives—that it helped them acquire the confidence and skills that they needed for success in college and careers. Scores of our graduates have overcome tremendous obstacles to become journalists, writers, and novelists. They include National Book Award finalist and MacArthur Fellowship winner Edwidge Danticat, novelist Ernesto Quinonez, writer Veronica Chambers, and *New York Times* reporter Rachel Swarns. Hundreds more are working in law, business, and other careers. Many are teachers, principals, and youth workers, and several have started nonprofit youth programs themselves and work as mentors—helping another generation of young people develop their skills and find their voices.

Youth Communication is a nonprofit educational corporation. Contributions are gratefully accepted and are tax deductible to the fullest extent of the law.

To make a contribution, or for information about our publications and programs, including our catalog of over 100 books and curricula for hard-to-reach teens, see www.youthcomm.org

About The Editors

Hope Vanderberg was the editor of *New Youth Connections*, Youth Communication's magazine by and for New York City teens, from 2004 to 2008.

Prior to working at Youth Communication, Vanderberg specialized in science journalism and environmental education. She was an editor at Medscape.com, a medical website, wrote articles for *Audubon* and *The Sciences* magazines, and taught children and teens at environmental education centers in California and Texas. She has also worked as a field biologist, studying bird behavior in Puerto Rico.

She has a master's degree in science and environmental journalism from New York University and a bachelor's degree from Earlham College. She is currently a freelance editor.

Keith Hefner co-founded Youth Communication in 1980 and has directed it ever since. He is the recipient of the Luther P. Jackson Education Award from the New York Association of Black Journalists and a MacArthur Fellowship. He was also a Revson Fellow at Columbia University.

Laura Longhine is the editorial director at Youth Communication. She edited *Represent*, Youth Communication's magazine by and for youth in foster care, for three years, and has written for a variety of publications. She has a BA in English from Tufts University and an MS in Journalism from Columbia University.

More Helpful Books
From Youth Communication

The Struggle to Be Strong: True Stories by Teens About Overcoming Tough Times. Foreword by Veronica Chambers. Help young people identify and build on their own strengths with 30 personal stories about resiliency. (Free Spirit)

Starting With "I": Personal Stories by Teenagers. "Who am I and who do I want to become?" Thirty-five stories examine this question through the lens of race, ethnicity, gender, sexuality, family, and more. Increase this book's value with the free Teacher's Guide, available from youthcomm.org. (Youth Communication)

Real Stories, Real Teens. Inspire teens to read and recognize their strengths with this collection of 26 true stories by teens. The young writers describe how they overcame significant challenges and stayed true to themselves. Also includes the first chapters from three novels in the Bluford Series. (Youth Communication)

The Courage to Be Yourself: True Stories by Teens About Cliques, Conflicts, and Overcoming Peer Pressure. In 26 first-person stories, teens write about their lives with searing honesty. These stories will inspire young readers to reflect on their own lives, work through their problems, and help them discover who they really are. (Free Spirit)

Out With It: Gay and Straight Teens Write About Homosexuality. Break stereotypes and provide support with this unflinching look at gay life from a teen's perspective. With a focus on urban youth, this book also includes several heterosexual teens' transformative experiences with gay peers. (Youth Communication)

Things Get Hectic: Teens Write About the Violence That Surrounds Them. Violence is commonplace in many teens' lives, be it bullying, gangs, dating, or family relationships. Hear the experiences of victims, perpetrators, and witnesses through more than 50 real-world stories. (Youth Communication)

From Dropout to Achiever: Teens Write About School. Help teens overcome the challenges of graduating, which may involve overcoming family problems, bouncing back from a bad semester, or even dropping out for a time. These teens show how they achieve academic success. (Youth Communication)

My Secret Addiction: Teens Write About Cutting. These true accounts of cutting, or self-mutilation, offer a window into the personal and family situations that lead to this secret habit, and show how teens can get the help they need. (Youth Communication)

Sticks and Stones: Teens Write About Bullying. Shed light on bullying, as told from the perspectives of the bully, the victim, and the witness. These stories show why bullying occurs, the harm it causes, and how it might be prevented. (Youth Communication)

Boys to Men: Teens Write About Becoming a Man. The young men in this book write about confronting the challenges of growing up. Their honesty and courage make them role models for teens who are bombarded with contradictory messages about what it means to be a man. (Youth Communication)

Through Thick and Thin: Teens Write About Obesity, Eating Disorders, and Self Image. Help teens who struggle with obesity, eating disorders, and body weight issues. These stories show the pressures teens face when they are confronted by unrealistic standards for physical appearance, and how emotions can affect the way we eat. (Youth Communication)

To order these and other books, go to:
www.youthcomm.org
or call 212-279-0708 x115

127